AF694628

The History of Computing

A lively and informative history of computing, starting with the early models of antiquity and continuing to today's modern computers. A look at the historical figures, inventions, discoveries and trends, all of which bring computing history to life.

edward franklin

ISBN: 978-1-77890-203-1
Imprint: Telephasic Workshop

Contents

Introduction

The Significance of Computing in Modern Society

Computing today is so pervasive that it can be said to underpin virtually every aspect of modern society. Computing technologies are essential for communication and information exchange, the operation of complex systems and processes, and even our everyday social interactions. It's hard to imagine the modern world without computers, and they influence virtually all aspects of our lives, ranging from economics and politics to culture and our personal interactions with each other. Computing is now central for anyone seeking to understand the modern world.

Overview of the Book

In The History of Computing, you'll dive deep into the past to track the evolution of computing from the Bronze Age to quantum computers. In this book, you'll encounter the historical giants who laid the groundwork for today's technologies and study the innovations, discoveries, trends and oddities of computer history, presented in storytelling form. Illustrated with captivating images, timelines and trivia, this book will whisk you on a suspenseful journey through the history of computing, covering both surface-level information and intriguing technical details. Whether you're a Silicon Valley veteran, a history buff, curious or just bored, this book will magically transport you to a world of historical computing, untangling the mysteries of our modern technology.

Early Foundations

Pre-Computing Devices

The modern computer belongs to a long line of computational devices that were created by human beings long before the invention of the integrated circuit. Some of the earliest mechanisms for computation date back thousands of years and the most elegant of these is the abacus. This section will trace the beginnings, operation and use of the abacus, putting this humble instrument in the context of the history of computing.

Abacus: The Ancient Calculator

The abacus is among the earliest known calculating instruments. It has played an important role in the historical development of mathematics and computing. In this section, we will cover the history, principles, and applications of the abacus.

History

The abacus dates back to ancient civilisations, specifically the Sumerians, Egyptians, Greeks, and Chinese. The word abacus is derived from the Greek 'abax', which means "accounting board". Ancient peoples used the abacus in slightly different forms, but the underlying principles remain unchanged. A version of this device popularised in the Western world is Chinese abacus, known as the suanpan. It consists of a wooden or metal frame containing usually two rods or wires on which beads are placed. Each rod or wire represents a place value, with the rightmost rod or wire representing the units place, and the next rod or wire the tens. Beads are moved along the rods to add or remove a quantity.

Principles

The abacus is based on the number system of place value and classical decimal arithmetic.

The beads on each rod represent a specific value, the lowest bead on the bottom rod representing the place values of the units, and the next below that, the hundreds, etc. Addition, subtraction, multiplication and division are performed on the abacus through the movement of the beads.

Addition is performed by moving the appropriate number of beads from the bottom, or units rod, to the desired place-value rods. To add five (5) and seven (7), the two beads on the bottom, five units, are moved from the rod to represent the appropriate number in the units place value spot (beads can really move like that!) and the two below that from the ten rods, show two spots, to get the answer of 12.

Subtraction is performed by moving beads the opposite of addition. To subtract three (3) from nine (9), a teacher demonstrates, you move three beads from the units rod to the empty spot to get the six (6) as the difference. The rules behind multiplication and division are certainly a bit more complex.

Multiplication is performed on the abacus through the movement of several beads many times at once. This helps to account for more than a one-digit operation, such as two times three is represented on the abacus by moving two on the bottom and moving three up to the thousands rods.

Division is a similar rule, only pairs of beads are moved to represent the dividend, and each subsequent product is placed underneath. When the quotient generates a remainder, it is placed in the units spot. Division is performed by the movement of beads a number of steps up the rods from the quotients and remainders.

Applications

Bookkeeping, commerce, trading and the teaching of mathematics are all practised and taught with the use of the abacus.

Moving the beads on an abacus can be used for simple and complex computation.

The abacus has been used in commerce and in economic activities since ancient times. Merchants and traders used it for bookkeeping and to keep inventory in ancient times. The use of the abacus brought to traders ease of use and quicker computation in their economic activities.

The abacus has been a useful educational tool. The abacus assisted those who wished to teach simple mathematics and computation.

In nearly every culture across the globe, the abacus is used as a learning tool for math. The presence of beads assisted those learning to visualize numbers and manipulate them; for small children, having physical beads assisted them with developing number sense.

The Greeks in ancient times taught their people to use the abacus. scholars in Europe in the Renaissance also learned the Greek method of using the abacus.

The abacus is still used in education today. Many schools and education programs throughout the world use the abacus as a learning tool.

Using the abacus improves a student's skills in number manipulation.

Example Problem

Let's consider an example problem to illustrate the use of the abacus for addition. Suppose we want to find the sum of 358 and 247 using the abacus.

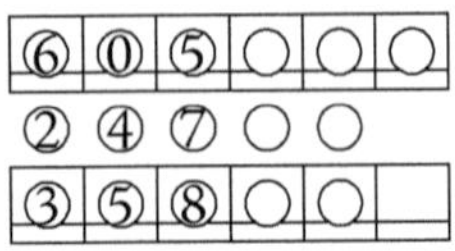

To add 358 and 247 on the abacus, we place the beads representing each digit on the respective rods. Starting from the units rod, we move beads to the left rods, carrying over when necessary. The final result is obtained by counting the beads on each rod:

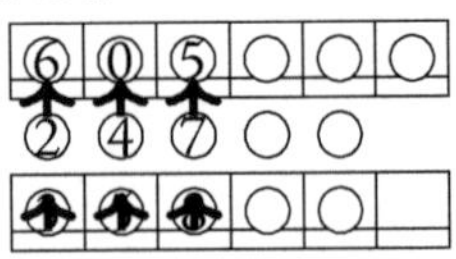

Thus, the sum of 358 and 247 is 605.

Conclusion

The abacus, one of the oldest human-built computers, is the best-preserved calculating tool in history. The abacus revolutionised calculation by employing place value and decimal arithmetic, and many aspects of modern computing are still rooted in these concepts. By using and analysing the abacus correctly, we can gain a deeper understanding of the origins of computing and the technological progress that has been made since its invention. And finally, the abacus is a testament to the human capacity for invention and problem solving: it is still used today to perform basic maths, and it is easy to use.

Antikythera Mechanism – A Peek Back Into the Past

The Antikythera Mechanism is the world's oldest analog computer, an ancient astronomical computer that relied heavily on ancient Greek engineering. This section dives into the specifications, function and principles that govern this ancient wonder.

Discovery and Specifications

The Antikythera Mechanism was discovered in 1901 by Greek sponge divers while searching for treasure on the seabed near the coast of the Antikythera island in the Aegean Sea, as described by Diogenes Laërtius.

The divers initially found the remains of a valuable cargo wreck but ended up salvaging a lump of corroded bronze from the seabed. They didn't think much of the bronze when they found it, possibly because the vessel Palanthos carried several remaining pieces of the mechanism.

The object transited several commercial routes before reaching the University of Chicago Oriental Institute in 1902, becoming part of the museum's collection. When F. M. Hoffman, a Swiss scholar, examined it five decades later, everything changed for ancient mechanics.

The Antikythera Mechanism is the most complex scientific object recovered from the ancient world. The surviving remains of this ancient computer exhibit extreme corrosion, making it hard to describe what it looked like before the onset of water damage. The extant fragments of the device, however, suggest that it was housed in a wooden box of the size of a shoebox. The front face contained several dials and some gears, while the rear was the face of gears.

Function and Operation

The function of the Antikythera Mechanism was not obvious, as it was heavily damaged. Due to the results of extensive analysis and still-going research, it is now clear that the mechanism is an ancient astronomical computer (calendar). The main dial on the front face of the device displayed a zodiacal calendar which showed the position at any given day and time of the Sun and other planetary bodies relative to the signs of the zodiac.

The gear train of the mechanism allowed the user to turn the harder (toothier) gears until the pointer on the dial moved to the current position of the Sun and other bodies. Other dials showed information such as the phases of the Moon and the dates of solar and lunar eclipses.

The gears of the Antikythera Mechanism performed complex calculations using gear ratios. These were combinations of gears of different diameters meshed together to apply a specific speed ratio. For example, if one gear had a diameter of 10 centimetres and the other 3 centimetres, and both teeth on each gear were the same height, then the smaller gear was meshed to the larger gear 33 times.

If the complete assembly moved or rotated, the smaller gear would spin five times faster than the larger gear. This was a nice way to subdivide a longer rotation into smaller intervals. A simple four-geared planetary gear train used a series of gears connected to each other with meshed teeth that all turned together, twisted together.

The original manufacturer of this ancient computer instrument had probably used information from known cycles of natural phenomena.

Three other gear systems were nested inside the initial set. This arrangement showed how these four bodies move in relation to the Earth and the Moon. This allowed them to trace the retrograde and prograde motions of Venus and Mercury, and the phases of the Moon.

Principles of Ancient Greek Engineering

The title of this section says it all. The Antikythera Mechanism shows that ancient Greeks could understand the astronomical movements of other celestial bodies and comprehend that the peaks of a phenomenon (solar eclipse, for example) provide information about the cycle and the next event. Therefore, they used a gear ratio mechanism to determine their calculation for the appearance. The principles used to build the Antikythera Mechanism are:

- Gear ratios.
- Knowledge of astronomy, geometry, mechanical engineering.

Interesting Side Note: The Olympic Games Indicator

The Olympiads were calculated from the first games in Olympia, which are dated to 776 BCE. This Olympiads indicator on the right side of the mechanism was not related to the other dials functionally. However, ancient Greeks could use the Olympics to figure out what year it was, what event was going on, and predict the time of the next Olympics. The extra feature of this ancient computer instrument shows the multi-discipline approach of ancient Greek engineering and that they integrated several types of knowledge into one instrument.

Further Reading and Resources

The topic of the Antikythera Mechanism is endless. Check out the following material to learn more about this amazing ancient computing machine.

- "Decoding the Heavens: A 2,000-Year-Old Computer–and the Century-Long Search to Discover its Secrets" by Jo Marchant.
- "The Antikythera Mechanism: A Concise Guide to the World's First Computer" by Yanis Bitsakis.
- The Antikythera Mechanism Research Project website (`http://www.antikythera-mechanism.gr/`)

These resources provide comprehensive insights into the history, construction, and ongoing research surrounding the Antikythera Mechanism, allowing readers to delve deeper into the realm of ancient Greek engineering and its remarkable contributions to the field of computing.

Early Numeric Systems

In the early days of computing, before the development of modern number systems, humans relied on various ancient numeric systems to perform calculations and represent numerical values. These early numeric systems laid the foundation for the mathematical principles that are still used in modern computing. In this section, we will explore some of the prominent early numeric systems and their significance in the history of computing.

The Babylonian Number System

The Babylonian civilization, dating back to around 2000 BCE, had one of the most advanced number systems of ancient times. The Babylonian number system was based on a sexagesimal (base-60) system, which is believed to have been influenced by their interest in astronomy and geometry. In this system, each position in a number represented a power of 60.

One unique aspect of the Babylonian number system was the use of a placeholder known as a "zero," which was represented by an empty space. This concept of zero as a placeholder was revolutionary and allowed for more complex calculations. The Babylonian number system also introduced the use of positional notation, meaning that the value of a digit depended on its position in the number.

To understand the Babylonian number system, let's take a look at an example:

$$37_{60} = (3 \times 60^1) + (7 \times 60^0) = 1800 + 7 = 1807_{10}$$

In this example, the number 37 in the Babylonian system is equivalent to 1807 in our modern decimal system.

While the Babylonian number system was primarily used for mathematical calculations, it also influenced the development of other ancient numeric systems, such as the Egyptian and Mayan systems.

The Roman Numerals

The Roman numerals are perhaps the most well-known ancient numeric system. Developed by the ancient Romans around the 9th century BCE, this system was primarily used for counting and recording numbers. The Roman numerals were based on a combination of letters from the Latin alphabet, with each letter representing a specific value.

The basic Roman numeral symbols are:

Symbol	Value
I	1
V	5
X	10
L	50
C	100
D	500
M	1000

To represent a number in the Roman numeral system, the symbols are combined, and their values are added together. However, there are some rules to follow:

- A smaller numeral placed before a larger numeral represents subtraction. For example, IV represents 4 (5 - 1) and IX represents 9 (10 - 1).

- A smaller numeral placed after a larger numeral represents addition. For example, VI represents 6 (5 + 1) and XI represents 11 (10 + 1).

- A numeral cannot appear more than three times in a row. To represent larger numbers, a bar is placed above a numeral to multiply its value by 1000. For example, V̄ represents 5000 (5 x 1000).

While the Roman numeral system was widely used in ancient Rome, it had limitations when it came to performing complex mathematical calculations. The lack of a zero placeholder and positional notation made it difficult to perform arithmetic operations efficiently.

Despite its limitations, the Roman numeral system continues to be used today in various contexts, such as in the representation of dates, the numbering of chapters and sections in books, and in the designations of monarchs and popes.

The Greek Attic Number System

The Greek Attic number system, also known as the Ionian or Milesian system, was used by the ancient Greeks from around the 5th century BCE. This system was primarily used for counting and recording numbers, similar to the Roman numerals.

In the Greek Attic system, each letter of the Greek alphabet represented a specific value. The basic symbols in this system are as follows:

Symbol	Value
☒	1
☒	5
Δ	10
☒	100
☒	1000

To represent a number, the symbols are combined, and their values are added together. However, similar to the Roman numeral system, there are rules to follow:

- A smaller numeral placed before a larger numeral represents subtraction. For example, ☒☒☒ represents 4 (5 - 1) and ☒☒☒ represents 9 (10 - 1).
- A smaller numeral placed after a larger numeral represents addition. For example, ☒☒ represents 6 (5 + 1) and Δ☒ represents 11 (10 + 1).
- A line drawn over a numeral multiplies its value by 1000. For example, ☒ represents 1000, while with a line over it (☒), it represents 1000000 (1000 x 1000).

Like the Roman numeral system, the Greek Attic system had limitations for performing complex mathematical calculations, mainly due to the lack of positional notation and zero as a placeholder.

Although the Greek Attic system is not widely used today, it played a significant role in the development of mathematical and scientific concepts in ancient Greece, contributing to the foundation of modern mathematics.

Conclusion

The early numeric systems, such as the Babylonian, Roman, and Greek Attic systems, played a crucial role in the development of mathematical concepts and principles that are vital to modern computing.

From the Babylonian system's introduction of zero as a placeholder and the use of positional notation to the Roman and Greek Attic systems' representation of numbers using letters, these ancient systems laid the groundwork for the more sophisticated numeric systems used in contemporary computing.

By understanding the origins of these early numeric systems, we can better appreciate the significance of the advancements made throughout the history of computing, leading to the development of the advanced numerical systems and algorithms used in modern computers.

Theoretical Foundations

Alan Turing's Contribution to Computability

However, one of the most profound breakthroughs in computing was made by another mathematician, the logician and Englishman of German descent Alan Turing.

Turing developed the mathematical foundations of computability, which defined what can and cannot be computed mechanically. His work, in papers such as On Computable Numbers, with an Application to the Entscheidungsproblem (1936), provided the foundation of the theory of computability and is therefore essential for any work on computing.

In this paper, he defines the concept of a universal machine, which would execute any computable procedure that could be represented in an algorithm. Modern machines known as universal Turing machines are named after his original concept.

See figure 1 for a depiction of a universal machine.

Figure 1. A block diagram of a universal machine (courtesy Wikipedia)

In modern terms, an algorithm is a step-by-step procedure for solving a problem. Turing proved that any computable procedure, which we now define as any procedure that can be carried out by an algorithm, can in fact be executed by a Turing machine.

He also proved that every computable function can be computed by an effective procedure – one that can be implemented by a human by following detailed instructions. The power of Turing's result lay in providing a mathematically precise definition of what could be computed, and what couldn't.

This result had a lasting impact on computing and inspired the work of philosopher Karl Popper, who in 1934 posed the question about the existence of a machine that could decide whether an abstract mathematical proof was correct or not. This question has come to be known as the Entscheidungsproblem – German for the decision problem.

Turing's solution solved the problem for good. Turing went on to work on other problems, such as the denial of unique factorisation of certain numbers into products of prime numbers, which mathematician David Hilbert had requested. He also made important contributions to the problem of undecidability and what came to be known as the halting problem. He proved that there are problems to which no algorithm can be applied that will tell us whether the problem associated with a given input will terminate. In that sense, he identified the limits of what can be computationally decided.

Although that problem might seem theoretical, it's worth emphasising that Turing played a key role in the Second World War as part of the group that broke the German Enigma code, arguably the most important intelligence victory of the war. The Enigma machine was an unbreakable cipher for transmitting encrypted messages such as orders and movements of military vessels. This work involved developing the first electronic computing machine, a device he called the Colossus, which was used to break the code.

In short, Turing's work laid the foundation for the machines of today and for computability theory in general.

To get a sense of Turing's insights for understanding what can and cannot be computed, let's examine the most famous example known as the halting problem.

The halting problem is concerned with the question of whether a given program will terminate for a particular input. Formally: 'Given a program P and an input I, is there a procedure that can decide if P will terminate on I?' Turing proved that there is no such procedure that can be applied to all programs and all inputs.

George Boole's Boolean Algebra

At the beginning of the 19th century, the English mathematician and philosopher George Boole invented a new system of algebraic logic, which is now called Boolean algebra. The study of this algebra became a major branch of mathematics based on binary variables, logical operations, and is an important basis for modern digital computers and electronic circuits.

Introduction to Boolean Algebra

Boolean algebra is a logic based on binary logic variables that can take on one of two values, true and false (writing 1 and 0 respectively) which can be interpreted as the two possible states of a pushbutton switch or equivalent component in an electronic circuit such as an ON and OFF position, or a HIGH and LOW voltage level.

Boolean algebra uses three basic logical operations to calculate a logical result from logical inputs, the three primary operations and their corresponding logic gates are: AND, OR, and NOT as depicted in Figure 9 below: Figure 9: Logical operations and logic gatesThe AND gate outputs true only if all its inputs are true (or false if all inputs are false), the OR gate outputs true if at least one of the inputs is true, and the NOT inverts its input and outputs the logical opposite of the input.SUMMARYTo combine any number of real variables (x,y,z) with logic operations, all of them must be represented using binary or Boolean variables (A,B,C) and the operations must be implemented by logic gates. Thus, x AND y means A AND B, the output A is the AND operation of the inputs of the AND gate.

Boolean Expressions and Truth Tables

Logical operations performed on variables are represented with symbols and formulas are known as Boolean expressions (a logical expression or a Boolean function), A Boolean expression is constructed only from variables representing the inputs of a logical operation, a logical operator symbol, and parentheses to indicate the order of the operation to be performed.

The behaviour of Boolean expressions is determined by making combinations of inputs for the variables in an expression and seeing the output for each combination, such behaviour is illustrated by a truth table showing the combination of all possible inputs in one row.

For example, let's consider the truth table for the Boolean expression A OR B:

A	B	A OR B
0	0	0
0	1	1
1	0	1
1	1	1

From the truth table, we can observe that the OR operation returns true (1) when at least one of the input variables is true.

Boolean Laws and Identities

Boolean algebra follows a set of laws and identities that govern the manipulation and simplification of Boolean expressions. These laws, also known as Boolean laws or Boolean identities, are derived from the properties of logical operations.

Some of the fundamental laws of Boolean algebra include:

1. Identity Laws: The OR operation with a true identity (1) returns the input variable ($A + 1 = A$), and the AND

operation with a true identity (1) returns the input variable ($A \cdot 1 = A$).

2. Null Laws: The OR operation with a null identity (0) returns the other input variable ($A + 0 = A$), and the AND operation with a null identity (0) returns 0 ($A \cdot 0 = 0$).

3. Domination Laws: The OR operation with a true value (1) returns 1 ($A + 1 = 1$), and the AND operation with a true value (1) returns the other input variable ($A \cdot 1 = 1$).

4. Idempotent Laws: Repeated application of the OR operation or the AND operation to a variable does not change its value ($A + A = A$ and $A \cdot A = A$).

5. Complement Laws: The NOT operation applied twice to a variable returns the variable itself ($\overline{\overline{A}} = A$).

6. De Morgan's Laws: The complement of the OR operation between two variables is equivalent to the AND operation of their complements ($\overline{A + B} = \overline{A} \cdot \overline{B}$), and the complement of the AND operation between two variables is equivalent to the OR operation of their complements ($\overline{A \cdot B} = \overline{A} + \overline{B}$).

These laws allow for the simplification and manipulation of complex Boolean expressions, making them more manageable and efficient in practical applications.

Digital Circuits and Boolean Algebra

Boolean algebra forms the foundation for designing and analyzing digital circuits, which are the building blocks of modern electronic devices and computers. Digital circuits consist of interconnected electronic components that perform logical operations on binary inputs to produce binary outputs.

Logic gates are the basic components of digital circuits, and they implement Boolean operations. The most common logic gates are the AND gate, the OR gate, and the NOT gate. These gates take one or more input signals and produce an output signal based on the Boolean operation they represent.

For example, an AND gate takes two input signals and outputs a logical true (1) only when both inputs are true. The truth table for an AND gate is:

A	B	A AND B
0	0	0
0	1	0
1	0	0
1	1	1

By combining logic gates, more complex circuits can be built to perform arithmetic operations, control flow, and memory functions, among other tasks.

Applications of Boolean Algebra

Boolean algebra has numerous applications in various fields, including computer science, electrical engineering, and digital electronics. Some notable applications include:

- Logic design: Boolean algebra is used to design and analyze digital circuits, allowing engineers to create complex systems from simple logic gates.

- Computer architecture: Boolean algebra plays a vital role in the design and operation of computer processors, memory systems, and input/output devices.

- Switching theory: Boolean algebra is used to model and analyze the behavior of digital switches and relay circuits, leading to advancements in telecommunications and automation.
- Computer programming: Boolean logic forms the basis for programming constructs such as if-else statements, loops, and conditional expressions.
- Robotics and automation: Boolean algebra is used to model and control robotic systems and automate industrial processes.
- Cryptography: Boolean algebra is employed in encryption algorithms and protocols to secure communication and protect sensitive information.

Boolean algebra continues to be a fundamental tool in the development of modern technologies, and its applications are pervasive in our digital world.

Summary

George Boole's development of Boolean algebra revolutionized the field of mathematics and laid the foundation for modern computing. Boolean algebra is based on binary variables and logical operations, which are represented by symbols and formulas in Boolean expressions. Truth tables are used to understand the behavior of Boolean expressions.

Boolean laws and identities govern the manipulation and simplification of Boolean expressions, allowing for efficient computation and analysis. Boolean algebra is widely used in digital circuit design and analysis, computer architecture, computer programming, robotics, cryptography, and other fields.

Understanding Boolean algebra is crucial for anyone working in the field of computing or engineering, as it provides the necessary tools to design and analyze complex digital systems. By mastering Boolean algebra, one gains the ability to harness the power of binary logic and contribute to the ongoing evolution of computing.

Charles Babbage's Analytical Engine

In the early 19th century, Charles Babbage, an English mathematician, engineer, and inventor, made significant contributions to the field of computing with his design for the Analytical Engine. The Analytical Engine was a proposed mechanical general-purpose computer that had the potential to perform a wide range of complex calculations. Although the Analytical Engine was never built during Babbage's lifetime, its design laid the foundations for modern computing.

Design and Features of the Analytical Engine

The Analytical Engine could store data and run instructions, enable arithmetic operations and chain instructions. It was governed by exceptionally modern design features. It included a stored program and separate memory and processing units, a distinct unit for every operation, and a way to defer execution of an operation until a particular data value was generated. All of these were significant features that were a clear step toward the modern computer.

Another important design feature of the Analytical Engine that was far ahead of its time was the use of separate memory and instructions – the principle of stored-program computing. The ability to store instructions and data separately, sequentially and recursively is an essential design feature of modern computers. Babbage also used punched cards for input and output. The input cards contained commands and data, while the output cards contained the results of the calculations. As a legacy from the punched card industry, the first wide-ranging computers also used punched cards for input and output.

A third design feature that was part of the Analytical Engine and also anticipates the modern computer is the use of conditional branching and looping. Babbage's Analytical Engine was intended to execute 'if-then-else' branches and 'loops' – repeating sections of instructions until a certain condition was reached. Control flow is the heart of all modern programming: in future computer designs, it would be achieved through jumps and branches in the logical execution control of the processor.

Despite its groundbreaking design features, Babbage was able to conceive a machine that was still mechanical in its functioning, in that it was based on the 'movement and monotonous vibration' of gears and levers. The Analytical Engine could multiply, add, subtract, take roots, and compute whole numbers. It could also perform logical operations such as negation and implication.

However, Babbage also included a way to represent non-integer numbers, including real numbers, so-called 'floating-point arithmetic'. He also gave a hint of the principles underlying electronic computers by describing mechanical logic gates, a method to perform computations using purely mechanical means.

Challenges and Limitations

Nevertheless, as with most breakthrough ideas, the Analytical Engine and its design fell victim to a combination of challenges and limitations that rendered completion in Babbage's lifetime impossible. The available mechanical engineering technology was from the start woefully inadequate.

The machine's several thousands of moving parts required an engineering control precision and tolerances that industrial manufacturing techniques could not provide. From geometric errors in the manufacture of components to insufficient application of lubricants and tolerances, many obstacles along Babbage's way were impossible to overcome.

Lack of financial resources was a huge concern. Babbage was conventionally dependent on the British government's funding to produce his design, and the adverse effect of his numerous design changes and needs must have taken their toll on government's appetite to provide the sustained funding he needed.

He never saw a penny (pound in British money) enough to realize his design. There was also the societal attitude to computing and understanding of its possible applications. Most people were yet to develop an appreciation for the overall impact such a machine could cause on science, engineering and commerce.

Legacy and Impact

Although never built, the Analytical Engine was the first design that had all the features required for a general-purpose computer. Thus, Babbage's concept helped to pave the way for future developments in computing, and influenced generations of inventors and engineers. Some even credit Babbage as the father of modern computing.

The most important document featuring his work was the algorithm written by the English mathematician and writer Ada Lovelace. Her notes were possibly the first algorithm ever conceived, and they vividly highlighted that the Analytical Engine could do much more than crunch numbers: Babbage took the first steps, letting us see to the heart of the modern computer's operations, to punch card tabulation equipment, to digital computers in general ...It is thus the father of all modern computers.

The tabulation system spurred by the study of the Analytical Engine led to the invention of punched card machines by Herman Hollerith. Hollerith's machines were used in the 1890

US Census, which had a population size of more than 62 million. The speed gain from using tabulation machines was enormous, making it one of the most important milestones in data processing and the ultimate step towards modern computers.

To this day, the principles of the Analytical Engine influence the architecture of contemporary computing and Babbage's work is still seen as a milestone in computing, even though his machine was never built. His attention to issues such as storage, memory, the difficulty of data access, and control mechanisms laid the groundwork for modern computers to become the most important tool in society today.

Ada Lovelace and the First Algorithm

Ada Lovelace, born as Augusta Ada Byron in 1815, is often referred to as the world's first computer programmer. She was the only legitimate child of the famous poet Lord Byron and a highly educated mother, Lady Anne Isabella Noel Byron. Ada's strong influence on early computing stemmed from her collaboration with the renowned mathematician Charles Babbage.

Ada Lovelace's Background and Contribution

Ada Lovelace's interest in mathematics and science developed from an early age. Her mother, concerned about her potentially inheriting her father's poetic temperament, encouraged her to focus on logic and reason. Lovelace excelled in mathematics and gravitated towards the subject.

In Lovelace's teenage years, she encountered both the mathematician and logician Augustus De Morgan and the mechanical engineer Charles Babbage. These encounters would shape her contribution to computing.

Charles Babbage's Analytical Engine

Charles Babbage is known as the "father of the computer" due to his conceptualization of the Analytical Engine, a mechanical general-purpose computer designed to perform various calculations. The Analytical Engine incorporated many innovations that would later become fundamental to modern computing, such as separate storage and processing units, a punch card system, and loops for repetitive tasks.

Although Babbage never fully constructed the Analytical Engine, he did outline its design. Lovelace was introduced to Babbage's work and became captivated by his ideas.

Ada Lovelace's Collaboration with Babbage

Ada Lovelace's work with Charles Babbage began in the mid-1830s and culminated in her translation of an article in 1840 for an issue of Taylor's Science Magazine about Babbage's Analytical Engine (written by the Italian mathematician Luigi Menabrea).

In her comprehensive notes, which should be read in conjunction with Menabrea's article, she formulated an extraordinary notion: the machine could be adapted to process not only numbers but also symbols and generate music, drawings and perhaps even artificial intelligence. Now known as the 'first computer programmer', Lovelace blazed the trail for using computers not simply for number-crunching but also for software and creativity.

Ada Lovelace's Algorithm

Ada Lovelace's most remarkable contribution was an algorithm that she formulated for Babbage's Analytical Engine so as to calculate a sequence of Bernoulli numbers. The command formulates a step-by-step set of instructions for solving the problem. In today's terms, it would be written in a programming language like the Python programming language.

The Significance of Ada's Notes

It became clear later just how crucial her contributions were. For more than 100 years, her notes were hidden away, unknown from the general public. In them is an algorithmic formulation of what might be the first computer program, a proto-software, the first programmable instructions for a computational machine. This impact of her work on the field of computing stayed hidden for decades. Indeed, it was only with the invention of the electronic stored-program computer in the early 1940s that the full ramifications of Lovelace's thinking could be appreciated.

In the 1980s, she was posthumously awarded the title 'first computer programmer' and became a feminist icon and role model for all girls interested in pursuing STEM subjects. Looking back, it seems remarkable that a woman could have produced such a text – which suggests that women have been 'doing things differently' all along.

Lovelace conceived an inspiring vision of what a machine was capable of. She saw that its potential lay not only in processing numbers. Recognising that computer programs could operate on symbols, as well as numbers, she imagined machines that would make music and generate imagery, not only sequence numbers.

Babbage envisioned a special-purpose steam engine for scientific calculation. Lovelace, in her own right, saw that computers could, in principle, be general-purpose machines, serving a wide array of purposes, not only mathematical such as trigonometry and probability. She hoped they could simulate a wide variety of computations, and even entertain or be a prank. Her algorithmic solution shows a pioneering approach for creating complex programs.

Babbage conceived of a mechanical machine; Lovelace, more creatively, envisioned a computer program – perhaps it was her first inkling that computational objects might be stored and executed entirely inside the machine. '[M]ay we not hope that machines will eventually compose music of some kind and even embody dramatic fancies of some sort'

She visualised the creative potential of the machine, yet had no intuition about the value of storage. Computers of today must not only process numbers, they must also store them – she came so close to formulating the concept! Her notes also hold a profound vision of a general-purpose machine capable of universal computing.

The modern idea of a general-purpose computer in which all problems can be solved on the same machine results from the extraordinarily fruitful imagination of Ada Lovelace.

Contemporary Relevance and Future Hope

In today's digital era, Ada's visionary ideas about what is possible on Babbage's Analytical Engine stand the test of time.

Her brilliant algorithmic solution shows that designing programs for computers requires a logical, step-by-step approach so that machines perform the task perfectly – a sober realisation that continues to inform all programming today. Moreover, Lovelace's expression of the creative potential of the computer is as inspiring today as it was in the 19th century.

Her famous note about the day machines will make music, as well as perform other fanciful activities, reminds us that computers can traverse a vast array of beautiful sonic structures and imagery. She believed that machines deserve our creative imagination.

True to her own words, Machines to compose Music of some kind, most certainly yes! Everything we tend to do contemporarily with computers, Ada had in mind 150 years ago. Her note expresses an unparalleled manifesto for the creative potential of the machine. Indeed, her enduring vision now seems truly omnipresent. With the help of machine learning algorithms, computers can create art that rivals that of great human artists.

Finally, Ada could not have anticipated how her suggestions of incorporating a nervous system into the Analytical Engine might be realised through the medium of neuromorphic computing. There is no reason to doubt Lovelace's belief that computers could embody artificial intelligence – what for her was just a joke could one day become reality.

Conclusion

Ada Lovelace's collaboration with Charles Babbage and her insightful writings laid the foundation for modern computing. Her algorithmic approach and visionary ideas anticipate many concepts we now take for granted, and her impact is felt to this day.

Lovelace's work serves as an inspiration to current and future generations of computer scientists and programmers, demonstrating the power of innovation and the significant role that creativity and logical thinking play in advancing technology.

As we explore the history of computing, it is essential to acknowledge and celebrate the remarkable contributions of Ada Lovelace, the world's first computer programmer, who shaped the field and set the stage for an ongoing revolution in computing.

Difference Engine: Babbage's Unfinished Project

Charles Babbage, often referred to as the "father of the computer," was a brilliant mathematician and inventor who made significant contributions to the field of computing. In the early 19th century, Babbage designed a mechanical device called the Difference Engine, which was intended to automate the computation of mathematical tables. This section explores the concept and design of Babbage's Difference Engine and the reasons behind its unfinished status.

The Need for Accurate Mathematical Tables

Before the advent of computers, mathematicians and scientists relied heavily on manually calculated mathematical tables for various computations. These tables were essential for calculations involving logarithms, trigonometry, and other complex functions. However, these calculations were prone to human errors and were time-consuming, often taking years to complete.

Recognizing the need for accurate and efficient methods for generating mathematical tables, Babbage conceived the idea of a machine that could automate these calculations, thus eliminating errors and greatly reducing the time required to produce the tables.

Principles of the Difference Engine

The key principle behind the Difference Engine was the method of finite differences. This method, first developed by the mathematician Johann Faulhaber in the 17th century, allowed the calculation of polynomial functions using a table of finite differences. By exploiting the regularity of these differences, Babbage aimed to simplify and automate the computation process.

The Difference Engine consisted of a series of interconnected cogwheels, gears, and cylinders, controlled by a system of levers. It utilized the method of finite differences to compute and print values of polynomial functions. Users would input the desired function into the engine, which would then use the method of finite differences to calculate the corresponding table of values.

Design Challenges and Technical Limitations

While the concept of the Difference Engine was innovative and promising, its development faced numerous challenges and technical limitations. One of the main difficulties was the precision required for the intricate mechanical parts. Babbage insisted on a high level of accuracy, which made the construction of the machine complex and costly.

Another significant challenge was the coordination of the numerous moving parts. The design involved a large number of gears and linkages, which had to be synchronized to ensure precise calculations. Achieving this level of coordination proved to be a formidable task, pushing the limits of engineering capabilities at the time.

Furthermore, the construction of the Difference Engine required substantial financial resources, which Babbage struggled to secure. The British government initially supported Babbage's project but later withdrew their funding due to budget constraints and concerns about the engine's practicality.

Unfinished Project and its Legacy

Despite his relentless efforts, Babbage was unable to complete the construction of the Difference Engine during his lifetime. Only a small portion of the machine was ever built, and it remained a symbol of ambition and unrealized potential.

However, Babbage's work on the Difference Engine laid the foundation for future computing advancements. The principles and concepts developed by Babbage were revolutionary and set the stage for the emergence of modern computers. His ideas influenced subsequent generations of engineers and inventors, inspiring them to explore new possibilities in computing.

Contemporary Relevance

Although Babbage's Difference Engine was never fully realized, its significance is still relevant today. The project highlighted the challenges faced in developing complex machines and the need for precision engineering. It also demonstrated the importance of securing adequate funding and resources to bring ambitious projects to fruition.

The legacy of the Difference Engine can be seen in modern computing, where complex calculations that once took years to complete can now be performed in a fraction of a second. Babbage's vision of automating mathematical computations laid the groundwork for the evolution of computing machinery, ultimately leading to the powerful computers we use today.

Exercises

1. Research and describe another early computing device that sought to automate mathematical computations. 2. Discuss the impact of Babbage's unfinished projects on the development of the computer industry. 3. Calculate the first five values of a given polynomial function using the method of finite differences. 4. Investigate the current state of Babbage's Difference Engine and any efforts to reconstruct or complete it. 5. Debate the benefits and drawbacks of using mechanical devices for complex calculations compared to modern electronic computers.

Resources

1. Swade, D. (2001). "The Difference Engine: Charles Babbage and the Quest to Build the First Computer." Penguin Books. 2. Lavington, S. H. (1998). "A History of Manchester Computers." The British Computer Society. 3. Baron, C. (1992). "Machines, Languages, and Computation: A History of Theoretical Computer Science." The MIT Press. 4. Hyman, A. (1982).

"Charles Babbage: Pioneer of the Computer." Princeton University Press.

Further Reading

1. Collier, B. (2013). "The Difference Engine: Charles Babbage and the Quest to Build the First Computer." Crown Publishing Group. 2. Campbell-Kelly, M. (2003). "The History of Mathematical Tables: From Sumer to Spreadsheets." Oxford University Press. 3. Bromley, A. G. W. (2010). "Charles Babbage's Analytical Engine, 1838." IEEE Annals of the History of Computing, 32(1), 66-71. 4. Randell, B. (1982). "Charles Babbage." In Copeland, B. J. (Ed.), "The Essential Turing: Seminal Writings in Computing, Logic, Philosophy, Artificial Intelligence, and Artificial Life, plus the Secrets of Enigma." Oxford University Press.

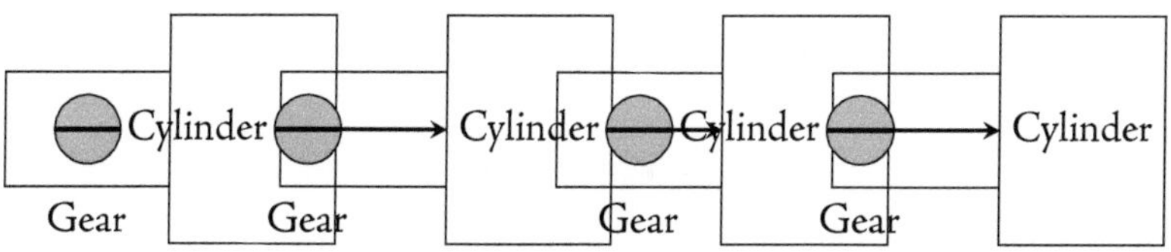

Figure 0.1: Simplified diagram of Babbage's Difference Engine.

Mechanical Marvels

Jacquard Loom

Hollerith's Tabulating Machine

Birth of Punch Card Systems

The development of punch card systems marks a significant milestone in the history of computing. Punch cards revolutionized the way data was processed and stored, setting the stage for modern computer systems. In this section, we will explore the birth of punch card systems, their impact, and how they paved the way for future advancements in computing.

The Need for Data Processing

As businesses and organizations grew in scale and complexity, there emerged a need for efficient data processing methods. Manual data entry and calculation were time-consuming and prone to errors. The inventors of punch card systems recognized the importance of automating these tasks to improve efficiency and accuracy.

Herman Hollerith and the Tabulating Machine

The American engineer and inventor Herman Hollerith was an early trailblazer of punch card systems. In the 1880s, Hollerith was asked to develop a system to process census data more rapidly. With the 1890 United States census around the corner, Hollerith was sent to textile mills to interest industrialists in his large punched cards.

The principle behind the weaving machine provided an inspiration: to make information available for tabulation faster and more accurately.

Hollerith's manuscript collection from 1880-1930, along with an electric tabulating machine type 1062 and a power governor, are held by the Smithsonian's National Museum of American History in Washington, DC. Each punched hole on one of Hollerith's cards encoded an item of data, such as a demographic or economic attribute about someone.

Birth of Punch Card Systems

The punch card system developed by Hollerith utilized a combination of mechanical and electrical components. Here's a step-by-step overview of the birth of punch card systems:

1. Data Entry: The process began with the manual entry of data onto punch cards. Trained operators used keypunch machines to punch holes in the appropriate positions on the cards.

2. Tabulating Machine: Hollerith's tabulating machine was designed to read and process the punched cards. It consisted of a series of electromechanical components that could detect the presence or absence of holes in specific positions on the card.

3. Sorting and Counting: The tabulating machine sorted the punched cards based on the presence or absence of holes in predetermined positions. By passing the cards through a series of mechanical relays and electrical circuits, the machine could tally the occurrences of specific data points.

4. Printing of Results: Once the data was processed, the tabulating machine could generate printed reports summarizing the collected information. This automated process greatly accelerated data analysis and eliminated errors that were common in manual calculations.

Hollerith's punch card system drastically reduced the time and effort required for processing large volumes of data. It was also highly accurate, as the tabulating machine could reliably read the holes punched in the cards. This breakthrough not only revolutionized the field of data processing, but also had a profound impact on various industries and scientific research.

Impact and Legacy

The punch card system developed by Hollerith became the foundation for modern computing. Its impact can be seen in several key areas:

- Business Applications: Punch card systems were adopted by businesses for tasks such as payroll processing, inventory management, and customer data management. This marked the beginning of automated data processing in the business world.

- Scientific Research: The ability to process and analyze large volumes of data quickly and accurately revolutionized scientific research. Punch card systems were used in fields such as astronomy, genetics, and social sciences to analyze vast amounts of data.

- Computing Infrastructure: The success of punch card systems laid the groundwork for the development of more advanced computing infrastructure. The concepts and principles behind the use of punched cards were later incorporated into early computer systems, such as the UNIVAC and IBM mainframes.

The birth of punch card systems not only transformed data processing but also paved the way for innovations in computer technology. The foundational concepts of automated data entry, efficient storage, and fast processing are still essential in today's computing landscape.

Unconventional Example: The Hollerith Codebreaker

While punch card systems were primarily used for data processing, they found an unexpected application during World War II. British codebreakers at Bletchley Park, including the famous mathematician Alan Turing, utilized Hollerith punch card machines in deciphering encrypted German messages.

By analyzing the frequency of German phrases and patterns, the codebreakers used Hollerith machines to generate statistical reports. These reports provided valuable insights and helped in cracking the German Enigma cipher. This unconventional use of punch card systems demonstrated their versatility and adaptability beyond their original purpose.

Further Reading

For those interested in diving deeper into the history and significance of punch card systems, the following resources are recommended:

- Book: "The Tabulating Machine: Technology and Organization" by Martin Campbell-Kelly

- Article: "Punched Card Systems and the Early Information Explosion, 1880–1945" by Richard W. Lyman
- Documentary: "The Computers" (2014) - a PBS documentary that explores the history of early computing, including punch card systems

These resources provide a comprehensive understanding of the birth of punch card systems and their broader impact on computing and society.

Mechanical Calculators

Pascal's Calculator

In the early days of computing, before the advent of electronic devices, mechanical calculators played a crucial role in facilitating complex calculations. One such remarkable invention was Pascal's Calculator, designed by the French mathematician and philosopher, Blaise Pascal, in the 17th century. The Pascaline, as it came to be known, was a mechanical device that streamlined arithmetic calculations, making them faster and more efficient.

Background

Blaise Pascal, born in 1623, showed exceptional mathematical aptitude from an early age. In 1642, when Pascal was just 19 years old, his father, a tax collector, sought his help in developing a device that could simplify repetitive calculations. The aim was to create a machine that could perform addition and subtraction with ease, alleviating the burden on the tax collector and reducing errors.

Design and Functionality

Pascal's Calculator, also known as the Pascaline, consisted of a box-like structure made of brass. It featured a series of numbered dials, gears, and mechanical wheels, which controlled the movement of the dials. The device resembled a modern-day odometer, where each dial represented a digit.

To perform addition, the user rotated the numbered dials using a stylus or pen, moving them forward or backward to represent the desired numbers. When the stylus was released, the dials locked into place, and the corresponding sum appeared through small windows.

The Pascaline had several innovative features that contributed to its functionality:

1. **Carry Mechanism:** Pascal's Calculator incorporated a carry mechanism, allowing the device to handle multi-digit calculations effectively. When a dial completed a full rotation, it triggered a carry-over to the next dial, similar to the concept of carrying over in manual arithmetic.

2. **Overflow Detection:** The device also featured an overflow detection mechanism that prevented the user from exceeding the maximum limit for each dial. As the user turned the dials, a mechanical stopper prevented further rotation past the dial's maximum value.

3. **Reset Function:** Pascal's Calculator included a reset function, allowing the user to quickly set all the dials back to zero for a new calculation. This feature saved time by eliminating the need to individually reset each dial.

Applications and Impact

Pascal's Calculator had a significant impact on mathematics, commerce, and science during its time. Its speed and accuracy made it a valuable tool for accountants, tax collectors, and merchants who relied on efficient bookkeeping. The device helped reduce calculation errors and increased productivity in various domains.

The Pascaline also provided a foundation for future mechanical calculators, inspiring further advancements in the field of computing. Other inventors and mathematicians, including Otto von Leibniz, built upon Pascal's work to develop more sophisticated calculating machines, eventually leading to the emergence of modern electronic computers.

Example Problem: Calculating Sales Totals

Let's consider a real-world example of how Pascal's Calculator could be used in a commercial setting.

Imagine a small shop owner who wants to calculate the total sales for the day. The shop sells various items, each priced differently. The owner needs to add up individual item sales to determine the total revenue generated.

Using Pascal's Calculator, the shop owner sets the first dial to represent the price of the first item sold. They repeat this process for each item, rotating the appropriate dial to the corresponding price. Once all the items have been accounted for, they read the sum of the sales from the dials to calculate the total revenue for the day.

The Pascaline's efficiency and ease of use would have made this task significantly faster and more accurate than manual calculations, benefiting small business owners and improving financial record-keeping.

Caveat

Despite its contributions to computing history, the Pascaline had some limitations. It could only perform addition and subtraction operations and was not capable of handling more complex mathematical calculations, such as multiplication or division. Additionally, the mechanical nature of the device made it prone to wear and tear, necessitating regular maintenance and repairs.

Further Reading

If you want to explore Pascal's Calculator and its impact on early computing further, the following resources provide more in-depth information:

1. Pascal's Calculator - The Pascaline (`https://history-computer.com/MechanicalCalculators/17century/Pascaline.html`): This website offers detailed insights into the design, functionality, and significance of Pascal's Calculator.

2. "Pascal's Calculator and the Pre-Digital Era" by Jean Marguin: This book delves into the history of Pascal's Calculator and its role in shaping the development of computing technology.

3. "The Universal Machine" by Ian Watson: This comprehensive book covers the history of computing from ancient times to the present, including a section on Pascal's Calculator and its impact.

Summary

Pascal's Calculator, or the Pascaline, was a pioneering mechanical calculating device invented by Blaise Pascal in the 17th century. It facilitated faster and more accurate addition and subtraction, improving efficiency in various domains such as commerce and mathematics. The Pascaline's technology laid the groundwork for subsequent advancements in the field of computing and was an important milestone in the history of calculators.

Through its innovative design features, including a carry mechanism, overflow detection, and reset function, Pascal's Calculator set the stage for the development of more sophisticated mechanical calculators. It played a crucial role in simplifying arithmetic computations and influenced the evolution of computing technology as we know it today.

Leibniz's Step Reckoner

In the early development of mechanical calculators, Gottfried Wilhelm Leibniz played a key role with his invention of the Step Reckoner. Leibniz, a German mathematician, philosopher, and polymath, designed this revolutionary device during the late 17th century. The Step Reckoner marked a significant advancement in the field of mechanical calculation and paved the way for future computing machines.

Motivation for the Step Reckoner

Leibniz was driven by the desire to create a machine that could perform complex calculations with high accuracy and efficiency. At the time, mathematicians and scientists relied on tedious and error-prone manual calculations. Leibniz recognized that a mechanical device capable of automating these calculations could dramatically improve scientific research, engineering, and various industries.

The Principle of the Step Reckoner

The Step Reckoner relied on the principle of mechanizing arithmetic operations using a stepped drum mechanism. Leibniz's design incorporated a series of numbered drums of varying sizes, each representing a different base. By rotating these drums, numbers could be displayed and manipulated. The larger drums represented higher digits, such as ones, tens, hundreds, and so on. Leibniz's innovative approach allowed for efficient calculation of large numbers.

Addition and Subtraction

To perform addition and subtraction with the Step Reckoner, Leibniz's design implemented a carry mechanism. When adding two numbers, each drum would display the sum of its associated digits. If the sum exceeded the base value of the drum, a carry would increment the next drum. Subtraction was achieved by complementing the number being subtracted and then performing addition using the carry mechanism.

Multiplication and Division

Multiplication and division on the Step Reckoner required a more intricate process. Leibniz devised algorithms for these operations, involving repeated additions and subtractions. He recognized that the efficiency of his machine would be limited by the time-consuming nature of these operations.

Accuracy and Limitations

Leibniz's Step Reckoner provided a significant advancement in calculation speed and accuracy compared to manual methods. However, the machine still suffered from some limitations. Mechanical tolerances and imperfections could introduce errors into calculations. Additionally, the limited number of digits that could be displayed on the drums restricted the range of numbers that could be handled.

Legacy and Impact

Although not widely adopted during Leibniz's lifetime, the Step Reckoner laid the groundwork for future mechanical calculators and computing machines. Leibniz's innovative ideas on the mechanization of calculation influenced subsequent inventors and engineers. The principles and concepts he introduced served as a foundation for the development of more advanced calculating devices in the centuries to come.

Example Problem: Multiplication using the Step Reckoner

Let's consider an example problem to illustrate the multiplication process on Leibniz's Step Reckoner. We want to calculate the product of 27 and 5 using this mechanical calculator.

1. Set the drums of the Step Reckoner to the digits of the multiplicand (27) and the multiplier (5). Align the drums properly, with the ones digit at the rightmost position.

7	2		5

2. Start with the rightmost digit of the multiplier (5). Multiply this digit by each digit of the multiplicand and record the results.

$$\begin{array}{r} 27 \\ \times \quad 5 \\ \hline 135 \end{array}$$

3. Move to the next digit of the multiplier. Multiply it by each digit of the multiplicand, taking into account the correct place value.

$$
\begin{array}{r}
27 \\
\times \quad 5 \\
\hline
135 \\
+ \quad 540 \\
\hline
1395
\end{array}
$$

4. Add up the partial products to obtain the final result. In this case, $27 \times 5 = 1395$.

Although this example might seem straightforward, the Step Reckoner provided a valuable tool for performing such multiplications more quickly and with fewer errors than manual methods.

Further Reading

If you would like to explore more about Leibniz's Step Reckoner and its significance in the history of computing, here are some suggested resources:

- "The Universal Computer: The Road from Leibniz to Turing" by Martin Davis.
- "The Calculating Machines (Die Rechenmaschinen): Their History and Development" by Ernst Martin.

These resources provide detailed insights into Leibniz's work, the Step Reckoner, and its impact on the development of computing machines. By diving deeper into the subject, you can gain a greater appreciation for the contributions made by Leibniz and the significance of his invention in the evolution of computing technology.

Summary

In this section, we explored Gottfried Wilhelm Leibniz's Step Reckoner, a mechanical calculator that revolutionized calculation during the late 17th century. We discussed the motivation behind its invention, the principles it relied upon, and its limitations. Furthermore, we worked through an example problem to illustrate the multiplication process on the Step Reckoner. Leibniz's invention served as a crucial stepping stone for future developments in the field of computing and laid the foundation for the machines we use today.

Difference Engines to Mechanical Calculators

In the early days of computing, before the invention of electronic computers, people relied on mechanical devices to perform calculations. This section explores the transition from difference engines to mechanical calculators, showcasing the advancements and innovations that paved the way for the modern computing era.

The Difference Engine

Charles Babbage, a British mathematician and inventor, is widely recognized as the pioneer of mechanical computing devices. In the early 19th century, Babbage designed the difference engine, a mechanical device capable of performing complex mathematical calculations.

The difference engine was designed to calculate and print tables of numbers, such as logarithm tables used in navigation and engineering. It employed a series of interconnected gears and levers to perform repetitive addition and subtraction operations. The machine used the method of finite-difference calculus to approximate the values of mathematical functions.

Despite its groundbreaking design, Babbage was unable to complete the construction of the difference engine due to various technical and financial difficulties. However, his ideas laid the foundation for future mechanical computing machines.

Mechanical Calculators

Following Babbage's work on the difference engine, other inventors and engineers continued to explore and develop mechanical computing devices. Several notable mechanical calculators emerged during this period, each with unique features and capabilities.

One such machine was Pascal's Calculator, invented by Blaise Pascal in the 17th century. This mechanical calculator used a series of gears and mechanical linkages to perform addition and subtraction. It was the first device of its kind that could perform calculations autonomously, without the need for external input.

Another influential mechanical calculator was Leibniz's Step Reckoner, invented by Gottfried Wilhelm Leibniz in the late 17th century. This device could perform all four basic arithmetic operations—addition, subtraction, multiplication, and division. It introduced a unique stepped drum mechanism that enabled automatic carry-over and enhanced calculation speed.

The development of difference engines and mechanical calculators ultimately led to the creation of machines that could perform more advanced tasks, such as solving complex equations and generating accurate tables of values.

Advancements and Challenges

While difference engines and mechanical calculators represented significant advancements in computing technology, they also faced several challenges and limitations.

One major challenge was the complexity and precision required in the construction of these machines. The intricate interplay of gears and linkages demanded a high degree of mechanical accuracy. Even minor imperfections in the manufacturing process could result in calculation errors or machine failure.

Additionally, the size and weight of these machines made them cumbersome and difficult to transport. This limited their practical use to specific applications and specialized environments, such as scientific laboratories and engineering workshops.

Furthermore, the input and output mechanisms of these early mechanical computing devices were relatively limited. Input was usually provided through mechanical dials, levers, or punched cards, while output was typically in the form of printed tables or mechanical displays.

Despite these challenges, the development of difference engines and mechanical calculators laid the groundwork for the future of computing. They demonstrated the feasibility of automating mathematical calculations and proved the value of mechanical devices in performing repetitive tasks efficiently.

Conclusion

The transition from difference engines to mechanical calculators marked a crucial phase in the evolution of computing. These early mechanical devices showcased the potential of automation and paved the way for future advancements in computing technology.

Although difference engines and mechanical calculators had their limitations, they set the stage for the advent of electronic computers and the computer revolution that followed. The principles and concepts developed during this period continue to influence modern computing systems and remain foundational to the field.

The journey from difference engines to mechanical calculators was a stepping stone towards the digital era we live in today. By understanding the rich history and struggles of early mechanical computing devices, we can gain a deeper appreciation for the remarkable progress made in the field of computing over the centuries.

The Electronic Era Emerges

ENIAC

UNIVAC

UNIVAC I's Impact on Elections

The UNIVAC I, developed by J. Presper Eckert and John Mauchly, was the first commercial electronic general-purpose computer. It was a groundbreaking technological achievement that had a significant impact on various aspects of society, including its role in elections. In this section, we will explore how the UNIVAC I changed the landscape of politics and the way elections were conducted.

The Pre-UNIVAC Era

Before the introduction of the UNIVAC I, elections were primarily conducted using manual methods. Counting and tabulating votes involved a laborious and time-consuming process. As the population grew and the complexity of elections increased, the need for faster and more accurate vote counting became evident.

The UNIVAC I: Revolutionizing Data Processing

The UNIVAC I, which stands for Universal Automatic Computer, introduced a new era of data processing. It was built with vacuum tubes and magnetic tape, allowing it to perform calculations faster and more efficiently than its predecessors. The computer had a memory capacity of 1,000 words, which was quite impressive for the time.

UNIVAC I and the 1952 U.S. Presidential Election

The UNIVAC I gained prominence for its role in the 1952 U.S. presidential election. The candidates were Dwight D. Eisenhower, a Republican, and Adlai Stevenson, a Democrat. The election was highly contested, and the outcome was uncertain.

The Pollster's Dilemma

The team behind the UNIVAC I saw an opportunity to garner attention and demonstrate the computer's capabilities. They approached the major television networks to showcase the use of the UNIVAC I in predicting the election results. However, the pollsters were skeptical, as they believed that the computer's predictions could be easily dismissed.

The Surprise Prediction

On election night, the UNIVAC I was put to the test. It was given data from early returns in key states and used its algorithms to make predictions. As the night went on, the computer generated results that were quite different from the predictions made by human pollsters.

The Network's Reluctance

The UNIVAC I's predictions were accurate and aligned with the final results of the election. However, the television networks were hesitant to report these results, as they preferred to rely on the expertise of the human pollsters. At that time, computers were still considered new and unproven in the field of predicting election outcomes.

A Historic Moment

Finally, at around 1:30 a.m., after the election had been decided, the UNIVAC I's prediction for the state of Pennsylvania was revealed on-air. It predicted an Eisenhower victory, countering the expectations of many viewers. This was a monumental moment in the history of computing and elections.

The Impact

The UNIVAC I's accurate prediction in the 1952 U.S. presidential election laid the foundation for the integration of computers in the electoral process. It demonstrated the potential for computers to analyze and process vast amounts of data to make predictions. It also highlighted the need for human trust and acceptance of computer-generated results.

Further Developments

Following the UNIVAC I's success, computer technology continued to advance rapidly, leading to the development of more sophisticated computers. The use of computers in elections evolved, with the introduction of electronic voting machines and more sophisticated data analysis techniques.

Contemporary Challenges

While computers have greatly improved the efficiency of electoral processes, they also present challenges. Concerns about the security and integrity of computerized voting systems have arisen, highlighting the importance of robust cybersecurity measures. Ensuring transparency and fairness in the use of computers in elections remains an ongoing challenge.

Conclusion

The UNIVAC I's impact on elections cannot be overstated. It changed the way we conduct elections, paving the way for the integration of computers in the electoral process. The accurate prediction made by the UNIVAC I in the 1952 U.S. presidential election was a defining moment in the history of computing and demonstrated the power and potential of computers in analyzing and processing data. As technology continues to advance, it is essential to address the challenges associated with the use of computers in elections to ensure the integrity and transparency of democratic processes.

UNIVAC and Early Commercial Computing

The development of UNIVAC marked a significant milestone in the history of computing, as it was the first electronic general-purpose computer designed for commercial applications. This section explores the impact of UNIVAC and early commercial computing on various industries and the growing trend of computerization in business operations.

UNIVAC I: From Military Applications to Business Computing

UNIVAC I, short for Universal Automatic Computer I, was developed by Eckert-Mauchly Computer Corporation (EMCC) in the early 1950s. It was the first computer designed to handle both scientific and business applications, making it a versatile machine for its time.

The construction of UNIVAC I was commissioned by the United States Census Bureau, primarily for processing census data. However, due to budget constraints, the Census Bureau had to cancel the project. Nevertheless, EMCC continued with the development and decided to target the commercial market instead.

In 1951, Remington Rand, a major manufacturer of business equipment, acquired the assets of EMCC and took over the production of UNIVAC I. The completed machine was delivered to the United States Bureau of the Census in 1951, becoming the first commercially available computer.

UNIVAC I's Impact on Elections

One of the notable early applications of UNIVAC I was in the prediction of the U.S. presidential election results in 1952. On the evening of November 4, 1952, UNIVAC I made history by successfully predicting that Dwight D. Eisenhower would win the election with a landslide victory.

UNIVAC I's prediction was based on a sample of just over 1% of the total votes recorded at that time. However, in an era where manual tabulation was the norm, the accuracy and speed of the UNIVAC I's prediction amazed many. This successful prediction played a crucial role in demonstrating the potential of computers for analyzing and processing large amounts of data.

UNIVAC and Early Commercial Computing

The success of UNIVAC I in predicting the election results led to a growing interest in using computers for a wide range of commercial applications. Private companies soon recognized the potential of computers to automate tasks, improve efficiency, and handle complex calculations.

Industries such as banking, insurance, and manufacturing were among the early adopters of computer technology. For example, banks started using UNIVAC I to automate bookkeeping, transaction processing, and customer account management. This improved accuracy, reduced manual errors, and saved considerable time and effort.

Similarly, insurance companies utilized UNIVAC I to perform actuarial calculations, assess risk factors, and process policy data efficiently. This enabled faster decision-making, streamlined operations, and improved customer service.

In the manufacturing sector, UNIVAC I facilitated inventory control, production planning, and quality control. By automating these processes, manufacturers could optimize their production, reduce costs, and improve overall efficiency.

Early Mainframes: IBM 700 Series

While UNIVAC I was making its mark in the commercial sector, IBM was also making significant strides in the field of computing. In the late 1950s, IBM introduced the IBM 700 series, a family of mainframe computers that further contributed to the advancement of commercial computing.

The IBM 704, part of the 700 series, was particularly important as it introduced the concept of floating-point arithmetic, which greatly enhanced the ability to perform scientific and engineering calculations. This made the IBM 704 a popular choice for scientific research institutions and engineering firms.

Moreover, the 700 series computers featured improved input/output capabilities, allowing them to handle a wider range of data processing operations. These mainframes became the workhorses of various industries, handling massive amounts of data and delivering reliable and efficient computing power.

DOS vs. Windows

In the early days of commercial computing, the operating systems used on these computers played a crucial role. Two significant operating systems emerged during this time: DOS (Disk Operating System) and Windows.

DOS, developed by Microsoft, was the dominant operating system during the 1980s. It provided a command-line interface and was mainly used for text-based tasks such as word processing and data entry. However, due to its limited graphical capabilities, DOS was not suitable for more visually-oriented applications.

Windows, on the other hand, was introduced by Microsoft in 1985 as a graphical user interface (GUI) for DOS. It provided users with a more intuitive and visually appealing way to interact with the computer. Windows quickly gained popularity and became the preferred operating system for commercial computing due to its ease of use and broader application compatibility.

IBM-Compatible PCs and Clones

As the demand for computers grew, IBM's approach to creating a closed, proprietary system faced competition from manufacturers producing IBM-compatible PCs. These IBM clones replicated the architecture and functionality of IBM's machines, offering more affordable options for businesses and consumers.

Competition in the PC market resulted in interoperability, as software and hardware designed for IBM machines could also run on IBM-compatible systems. This interoperability contributed to the rapid expansion of the commercial computing industry, with more software and peripherals becoming readily available to users.

The rise of IBM-compatible PCs and clones played a pivotal role in driving down costs, expanding the market, and establishing personal computing as a mainstream phenomenon. It fueled innovation, increased competition, and led to the diversification of computing platforms.

Conclusion

The development of UNIVAC and the growth of early commercial computing marked a significant transition in the evolution of computing. UNIVAC I's success in predicting the 1952 presidential election demonstrated the potential of computers in commercial applications, leading to increased interest and investment in computing technology.

The adoption of UNIVAC I and subsequent mainframe computers like the IBM 700 series by industries such as banking, insurance, and manufacturing brought about significant improvements in efficiency, accuracy, and decision-making. The introduction of operating systems like DOS and Windows provided users with more user-friendly interfaces and broader application possibilities.

The emergence of IBM-compatible PCs and clones further accelerated the adoption of computers in businesses and homes, making computing more accessible and affordable. This paved the way for the widespread use of computers in various industries and set the stage for the personal computing revolution.

As we continue the journey through the history of computing, the next section will explore the breakthroughs in electronic technology that brought about the miniaturization of computers and the birth of personal computing.

Early Mainframes: IBM 700 Series

The evolution of computing during the mid-20th century saw the emergence of mainframe computers, which played a vital role in business, scientific research, and government applications. One of the most significant series of mainframe computers during this time was the IBM 700 Series. In this section, we will explore the early mainframe computers developed by IBM, focusing on the IBM 701, IBM 704, and IBM 709 models.

The IBM 701: First Generation Mainframe

The IBM 701, introduced in 1952, marked IBM's entry into the mainframe computer market. It was the company's first commercially successful scientific computer. The IBM 701 utilized vacuum tubes for its logic circuits, offering speeds of around 5,000 instructions per second. Despite its relatively limited processing power and memory, the IBM 701 paved the way for future advancements in mainframe computing.

One of the notable features of the IBM 701 was its pioneering use of floating-point arithmetic. This allowed for more precise calculations, making it suitable for scientific and engineering applications. The system also had a drum memory unit, which provided faster access to data compared to earlier magnetic tape systems.

The IBM 704: Advancements in Architecture

Building upon the success of the IBM 701, IBM developed the IBM 704 in 1954. The IBM 704 featured several notable architectural advancements that contributed to its improved performance and flexibility.

One of the key innovations introduced in the IBM 704 was the concept of addressing. This allowed programmers to access specific sections of the computer's memory directly. The improved addressing capabilities, along with an expanded memory capacity, made the IBM 704 well-suited for scientific and engineering calculations.

Additionally, the IBM 704 introduced index registers, which greatly enhanced the ability to perform array processing and data manipulation. It also featured improved input/output capabilities, enabling faster data transfer between the computer and external devices.

The IBM 704 became widely adopted in various scientific and research institutions, playing a crucial role in fields such as physics, mathematics, and aerospace engineering.

The IBM 709: Transition to Transistors

In the late 1950s, IBM introduced the IBM 709, representing a transition from vacuum tube technology to transistors. The shift to transistors enabled significant improvements in performance, reliability, and power consumption.

The IBM 709 offered faster processing speeds, with the ability to execute approximately 120,000 instructions per second. It also featured an expanded memory capacity of up to 32,768 words, providing increased storage capabilities for complex scientific and business applications.

One of the notable advancements in the IBM 709 was the introduction of core memory. Core memory used an array of tiny magnetic cores to store data, offering faster access times and greater stability compared to drum or tube-based memories.

The IBM 709 enjoyed widespread adoption and was utilized in a wide range of applications, including weather prediction, atomic energy research, and defense-related calculations.

Legacy and Impact

The IBM 700 Series of mainframe computers played a crucial role in advancing the capabilities of computing during the 1950s and 1960s. These early mainframes laid the foundation for subsequent generations of computers, contributing to the growth of scientific research, industrial automation, and business computing.

The architectural innovations introduced in the IBM 700 Series, such as improved memory management, enhanced input/output capabilities, and the transition to transistor technology, set the stage for future advancements in mainframe computing.

The success of the IBM 700 Series also established IBM as a dominant player in the mainframe market, a position the company maintained for several decades. The influence of early mainframes like the IBM 701, IBM 704, and IBM 709 can still be seen in modern computing systems, showcasing the enduring impact of these pioneering machines.

Conclusion

The IBM 700 Series of mainframe computers introduced by IBM in the 1950s played a crucial role in the evolution of computing. From the IBM 701's pioneering use of floating-point arithmetic to the architectural advancements of the IBM 704 and the transition to transistors in the IBM 709, these early mainframes pushed the boundaries of what was possible in computing.

The developments made in the IBM 700 Series laid the foundation for future generations of mainframe computers, revolutionizing scientific research, industrial automation, and business applications. The legacy of these early mainframes can still be seen in the modern computing landscape, serving as a testament to the lasting impact of their innovations.

Transistors and Miniaturization

The Advent of Transistors

In the early days of computing, vacuum tubes were the primary electronic components used in computers. However, vacuum tubes were large, fragile, and consumed a lot of power. They were also prone to overheating and had a limited lifespan. These limitations made them impractical for mass-produced computers.

The invention of the transistor in 1947 revolutionized the field of electronics and paved the way for the development of smaller, faster, and more reliable computers. The transistor, a solid-state device made of semiconductor materials, acted as an amplifier and switch, performing the same functions as the vacuum tube but with significant advantages.

Principles of Transistors

Transistors are based on the principles of solid-state physics and utilize the properties of semiconductors to control the flow of electric current. A transistor consists of three layers of doped semiconductor materials: the emitter, base, and collector.

The behavior of a transistor is governed by the two main types: bipolar junction transistors (BJTs) and field-effect transistors (FETs).

Bipolar Junction Transistors (BJTs): BJTs are composed of two pn (positive-negative) junctions and can be classified into two types: NPN and PNP. NPN transistors have a negatively charged emitter and positively charged collector, while PNP transistors have a positively charged emitter and negatively charged collector. The current flow between the emitter and collector is controlled by the base current.

Field-Effect Transistors (FETs): FETs rely on an electric field to control the flow of current. They are composed of three terminals: the source, drain, and gate. FETs can be further classified into two types: N-channel and P-channel. In an N-channel FET, the channel has a majority of electrons, and the gate voltage controls the flow of electrons between the source and drain. In a P-channel FET, the channel has a majority of holes, and the gate voltage controls the flow of holes.

Advantages of Transistors

The advantages of transistors over vacuum tubes were numerous:

- **Size:** Transistors are much smaller than vacuum tubes, allowing for the development of miniaturized electronic devices and computers.
- **Reliability:** Transistors do not have moving parts like vacuum tubes, making them more resistant to shock and vibration. They also have a longer lifespan and do not suffer from the same overheating issues.
- **Power Efficiency:** Transistors consume significantly less power than vacuum tubes, resulting in more energy-efficient electronic devices.
- **Speed:** Transistors can switch on and off much faster than vacuum tubes, allowing for faster computational speeds.

Applications of Transistors

The invention of transistors opened up a world of possibilities for electronic devices and computers. They were quickly adopted in various fields, leading to significant advancements. Some notable applications include:

- **Computers:** Transistors enabled the development of smaller and more powerful computers. They replaced vacuum tubes, reducing the size and power consumption of computers while increasing their reliability and computational speed.

- **Communication Systems:** Transistors revolutionized communication systems, allowing for the development of smaller and more portable radios, televisions, and telephones. They also played a crucial role in the development of mobile and wireless communication technologies.

- **Consumer Electronics:** Transistors formed the foundation of various consumer electronics, including calculators, digital watches, and audio amplifiers. These devices became more affordable and widely available due to the use of transistors.

Challenges and Limitations

While transistors offered significant advantages over vacuum tubes, they still faced some challenges and limitations:

- **Heat Dissipation:** Transistors generate heat during operation, and efficient heat dissipation is critical to ensure their proper functioning. Overheating can lead to device failure and reduced lifespan.

- **Manufacturing Complexity:** The manufacturing process of transistors is complex and requires advanced techniques. Any defects or impurities in the semiconductor materials can affect the performance of transistors.

- **Physical Limitations:** As transistors continue to shrink in size, they approach physical limits imposed by quantum mechanics. This limits the ability to further miniaturize electronic devices and increase their computational speed.

Future Developments

Despite the challenges and limitations, transistors continue to play a vital role in modern electronic devices. However, researchers are exploring alternative technologies to overcome these limitations.

One promising direction is the development of **nanoscale transistors** using new materials and techniques to enhance their performance and energy efficiency. Another exciting avenue is the field of **quantum computing**, where quantum effects are harnessed to perform computations at a much higher speed than conventional computers.

By continually pushing the boundaries of transistor technology, researchers are striving to meet the growing demands of the digital age and pave the way for future advancements in computing and electronics.

Summary

In this section, we explored the advent of transistors and their impact on computing and electronics. Transistors revolutionized the field by offering smaller size, greater reliability, power efficiency, and increased speed compared to vacuum tubes. We discussed the principles of transistors, their advantages, and applications. We also highlighted the challenges and limitations faced by transistors and touched upon future developments in nanoscale transistors and quantum computing. Transistors remain a crucial component in modern electronic devices, paving the way for continued advancements in the field of computing.

Integrated Circuits: Shrinking the Computer

In the early days of computing, computers were massive machines that took up entire rooms. They were built using vacuum tubes and relied on bulky wiring systems. However, as technology advanced, the need for smaller and more efficient computers became apparent. This led to the development of integrated circuits, which revolutionized the field of computing by shrinking the size of computers and increasing their processing power. In this section, we will explore the concept of integrated circuits, their benefits, and their impact on the computer industry.

Introduction to Integrated Circuits

Integrated circuits, also known as ICs or microchips, are miniature electronic circuits made up of thousands or millions of transistors, resistors, and capacitors that are fabricated on a small semiconductor wafer. These components are etched onto the wafer using a process called photolithography. The result is a compact and highly efficient electronic device that performs various functions, such as processing, memory storage, and logic operations.

The development of integrated circuits can be attributed to the work of Jack Kilby and Robert Noyce in the late 1950s and early 1960s. Kilby, an engineer at Texas Instruments, developed the first working integrated circuit in 1958. Noyce, co-founder of Fairchild Semiconductor and later Intel, also independently developed the integrated circuit in 1959. Their groundbreaking inventions paved the way for the miniaturization of electronic components and the birth of modern computing.

Benefits of Integrated Circuits

The introduction of integrated circuits brought about significant advantages for the computer industry. Here are some key benefits of integrated circuits:

1. Miniaturization: Integrated circuits allowed computers to become much smaller and more portable. This advancement opened up new possibilities for personal computers, laptops, and, eventually, mobile devices.

2. Increased Processing Power: Integrated circuits enabled higher levels of integration, which meant more transistors could be packed into a smaller space. This led to a significant increase in processing power and improved the overall performance of computers.

3. Energy Efficiency: Compared to traditional vacuum tube-based computers, integrated circuits consumed significantly less power. This improvement in energy efficiency was a game-changer for portable devices, as it extended battery life and reduced the need for bulky power supplies.

4. Cost Reduction: As the manufacturing process for integrated circuits became more refined, the cost of producing them decreased significantly. This made computers more affordable and accessible to a wider range of users.

5. Reliability: Integrated circuits replaced fragile vacuum tubes with solid-state components, enhancing the reliability and durability of computers. This made them less prone to failures and reduced the need for frequent maintenance.

Fabrication of Integrated Circuits

The fabrication process of integrated circuits involves several complex steps, starting from the design phase to the final packaging of the microchips. Let's explore the key stages of integrated circuit fabrication:

1. Design: The first step in creating an integrated circuit is the design phase. Engineers use Computer-Aided Design (CAD) software to create a blueprint of the circuit, including the placement and interconnection of transistors, resistors, and capacitors.

2. Wafer Preparation: A semiconductor material, typically silicon, is prepared to create the wafer on which the integrated circuits will be built. The wafer is carefully polished to achieve a smooth surface.

3. Photolithography: In this crucial step, a layer of photosensitive material, known as photoresist, is applied to the wafer. A pattern mask is then used to expose specific areas of the photoresist to ultraviolet light. The exposed areas become soluble and are washed away, leaving behind a patterned layer.

4. Etching: The exposed areas of the wafer are etched using a chemical process or plasma etching. This removes the unwanted portions of the wafer, leaving behind the desired circuit pattern.

5. Deposition: Thin layers of various materials, such as conductive metals or insulators, are deposited onto the wafer using techniques like chemical vapor deposition or sputtering. These layers form the different components of the integrated circuit.

6. Etching and Deposition (Repeat): The process of etching and deposition is repeated multiple times to create the desired circuit structure. This allows for the formation of transistors, resistors, capacitors, and interconnects.

7. Testing: Once the fabrication process is complete, the integrated circuits need to undergo rigorous testing to ensure their functionality and performance. This involves electrical and functional testing using specialized equipment.

8. Packaging: The final step is packaging the integrated circuits. They are placed in protective casings and connected to external pins or leads to facilitate their integration into electronic devices.

Moore's Law: The Driving Force

When discussing integrated circuits and their impact on computer technology, it is impossible not to mention Moore's Law. Coined by Gordon Moore, one of the co-founders of Intel, in 1965, Moore's Law states that the number of transistors on an integrated circuit doubles approximately every two years. This observation has held true for several decades and has been a driving force behind the rapid advancement of computer technology.

Moore's Law has had profound implications for the computer industry. It has enabled the continuous improvement of processing power, memory capacity, and overall performance of computers. The relentless pursuit of smaller, faster, and more efficient integrated circuits has allowed computers to become more powerful yet smaller in size.

However, Moore's Law is not without challenges. As the number of transistors on an integrated circuit increases, it becomes increasingly difficult to maintain their performance while keeping power consumption and heat dissipation under control. This has led to the exploration of alternative technologies and approaches to continue pushing the boundaries of integrated circuit development.

Conclusion

Integrated circuits have played a pivotal role in revolutionizing the field of computing. They have allowed for the miniaturization of computers, increased processing power, improved energy efficiency, and reduced costs. The development and refinement of integrated circuits have been guided by Moore's Law, which has driven the continuous improvement of computer technology.

As technology advances, the demand for smaller, faster, and more powerful integrated circuits will continue to grow. The future of computing lies in the ongoing exploration of new materials, alternative fabrication techniques, and innovative approaches to overcome the challenges posed by Moore's Law. By harnessing the potential of integrated circuits, we can pave the way for a more connected, intelligent, and efficient future.

Microprocessors: Birth of Personal Computing

In the early days of computing, computers were massive machines that occupied entire rooms and were used mainly by large organizations and government institutions. However, in the 1970s, a major breakthrough occurred with the invention of the microprocessor, which paved the way for the birth of personal computing. This section explores the development of microprocessors and their impact on the computer industry.

The Advent of Microprocessors

The microprocessor is a key component of modern computer systems, acting as the central processing unit (CPU) that executes instructions and performs calculations. The development of the first microprocessor can be attributed to a team of engineers at Intel, led by Ted Hoff. In 1971, Intel introduced the 4004, the world's first commercially available microprocessor.

The Intel 4004 was a 4-bit processor designed for use in calculators and other small electronic devices. It featured 2,300 transistors and operated at a clock speed of 740 kHz. Although limited in performance compared to today's microprocessors, the 4004 was a groundbreaking development that revolutionized the computer industry.

Impact on Personal Computing

The introduction of microprocessors had a profound impact on personal computing, enabling the development of smaller, more affordable, and more powerful computers. Here are some key areas where microprocessors played a significant role:

Miniaturization and Portability: Microprocessors allowed computers to be significantly smaller and more portable than their predecessors. This led to the development of early personal computers that could fit on a desk or even be carried by an individual.

Affordability: The use of microprocessors made computers more affordable, as they were cheaper to produce and required less power to operate. This made personal computers accessible to a broader range of users and spurred the growth of the consumer market.

Increased Processing Power: Microprocessors brought significant improvements in processing power, allowing computers to perform complex tasks more efficiently. This advancement led to the development of software applications that were previously unimaginable, such as spreadsheets, word processors, and graphical user interfaces.

Expansion of Applications: The availability of microprocessors opened up new possibilities for computing applications. It enabled the integration of computers into various industries, including business, education, and entertainment. Microprocessors also facilitated the development of gaming consoles and home entertainment systems.

Moore's Law and the Evolution of Microprocessors

As microprocessors evolved, they followed a trajectory of exponential growth in terms of processing power and efficiency. This trend is often attributed to Moore's Law, which states that the number of transistors on a chip doubles approximately every two years.

Moore's Law, coined by Intel co-founder Gordon Moore in 1965, has held true for several decades, driving the advancement of microprocessors. Advances in semiconductor technology, such as improved manufacturing processes and smaller transistor sizes, have allowed more transistors to be placed on a single chip, resulting in increased computing power.

The continuous improvement in microprocessor performance has led to the development of faster and more capable computers. From the Intel 4004 to modern-day processors like the Intel Core i9, microprocessors have undergone numerous generations, with each iteration offering better performance, lower power consumption, and increased functionality.

Challenges and Future Trends

While microprocessors have played a vital role in the advancement of personal computing, their development has not been without challenges. As transistors approach atomic scale, several fundamental limitations have emerged.

One significant challenge is power consumption. As microprocessors become faster and more complex, they tend to consume more power, leading to increased heat generation and the need for more advanced cooling solutions. Furthermore, the shrinking of transistor sizes has introduced issues related to heat dissipation and electrical leakage.

Another challenge is the physical constraints of semiconductor technology. As transistor sizes continue to decrease, quantum effects begin to impact their behavior, leading to increased uncertainty and reduced reliability. These challenges necessitate the exploration of alternative technologies, such as quantum computing and novel materials, to overcome the limitations of traditional microprocessors.

Looking into the future, several trends are shaping the evolution of microprocessors. One such trend is the development of multi-core processors, which integrate multiple processing units on a single chip. This approach allows for parallel processing and improved performance in tasks that can be divided into smaller, concurrent threads.

Another trend is the increasing focus on energy efficiency. As computing devices become more pervasive in our daily lives, there is a growing demand for processors that consume less power and offer longer battery life. Power optimization techniques and innovative architectures are being explored to address this need.

Furthermore, the rise of artificial intelligence (AI) and machine learning has prompted the development of specialized processors, such as graphics processing units (GPUs) and tensor processing units (TPUs), designed to accelerate AI workloads. These processors leverage parallel processing and specialized architectures to deliver significant performance gains in AI applications.

In conclusion, the invention of the microprocessor marked a significant milestone in the history of computing, enabling the birth of personal computing. Microprocessors have continuously evolved, following Moore's Law, and have driven the advancement of computing power, portability, and affordability. However, future challenges related to power consumption and physical limitations necessitate the exploration of alternative technologies. The ongoing trends towards multi-core processors, energy efficiency, and specialized processors align with the growing demands of modern computing applications. The journey of microprocessors continues to shape the way we interact with computers and holds the promise of future innovations.

Birth of Personal Computing

Altair 8800: The First Personal Computer

Apple I and II

GUI and the Macintosh

The graphical user interface (GUI) revolutionized the way we interact with computers and played a crucial role in the success of the Macintosh, Apple's groundbreaking personal computer. In this section, we will explore the development of GUI and its impact on computing.

The Need for a User-Friendly Interface

Before the advent of GUI, computers were operated mainly through command-line interfaces, where users had to type complex commands to perform tasks. This approach required specialized knowledge and made computers accessible only to a limited number of users, such as programmers and engineers. The need for a user-friendly interface was evident as the demand for personal computers grew.

Xerox PARC and the Birth of GUI

The Xerox Palo Alto Research Center (PARC) played a pivotal role in the development of GUI. In the 1970s, a team of researchers led by Alan Kay and Douglas Engelbart at Xerox PARC envisioned a more intuitive and interactive way to use computers. They introduced several key concepts that formed the basis of GUI, including windows, icons, and pointing devices.

Macintosh and Lisa: Early GUI-based Computers

Apple was quick to recognize the potential of GUI and incorporated it into their Lisa computer, which was released in 1983. However, due to its high price, Lisa did not achieve widespread popularity. Undeterred, Apple continued to refine the concept of GUI and released the Macintosh computer in 1984.

Macintosh: Intuitive and User-Friendly

The Macintosh was revolutionary, thanks to its intuitive GUI and mouse-driven interface. It featured a desktop metaphor where users interacted with graphical representations of files, folders, and applications. This approach made it easy for non-technical users to navigate and perform tasks on the computer.

Graphical Elements of Macintosh GUI

The Macintosh GUI introduced several graphical elements that have become standard in modern user interfaces. These include the menu bar at the top of the screen, dropdown menus, scroll bars, and dialog boxes. The desktop also featured icons that represented files and applications, which could be opened by double-clicking.

WIMP: Windows, Icons, Menus, and Pointing Device

The Macintosh GUI popularized the WIMP paradigm, which stands for Windows, Icons, Menus, and Pointing Device. This paradigm revolutionized the way we interact with computers and laid the foundation for modern user interfaces. Windows allowed users to work with multiple applications simultaneously, while icons provided visual representations of files and applications. Menus offered a hierarchical structure for accessing commands, and the pointing device, usually a mouse, facilitated user input.

The Macintosh Effect

The Macintosh's user-friendly interface and intuitive design had a profound impact on the computing industry. It not only set a new standard for personal computer interfaces but also influenced the development of GUI in other operating systems. Microsoft later adopted many elements of the Macintosh GUI for their Windows operating system, making it accessible to a wider audience.

GUI Beyond Macintosh

The success of the Macintosh GUI opened doors for GUI-based development in various domains, such as multimedia, gaming, and design. Applications with graphical interfaces became more prevalent, enabling users to manipulate digital content with ease. GUI also paved the way for touch-based interfaces, which are now widely used in smartphones and tablets.

Further Readings and Resources

If you're interested in learning more about GUI and the Macintosh, here are some recommended resources:

- *Revolution in the Valley: The Insanely Great Story of How the Mac was Made* by Andy Hertzfeld.

- *The Innovators: How a Group of Hackers, Geniuses, and Geeks Created the Digital Revolution* by Walter Isaacson.
- *The Macintosh Way* by Guy Kawasaki.
- *Designing Interactions* by Bill Moggridge.

These books provide valuable insights into the people, ideas, and innovations that shaped GUI and its impact on computing.

Conclusion

The development of GUI and its implementation in the Macintosh computer transformed the way we interact with computers. It made computing accessible to a wider audience and set new standards for user-friendly interfaces. The Macintosh GUI influenced the design of modern operating systems and opened up new possibilities for intuitive user interaction. GUI continues to evolve, with touch-based interfaces now becoming commonplace. As we look to the future, GUI will undoubtedly play a crucial role in shaping the next generation of computing interfaces.

Apple's Impact on Home Computing

Apple Inc., founded by Steve Jobs and Steve Wozniak in 1976, has had a profound impact on the field of home computing. Their innovative products and user-friendly interfaces revolutionized the way people interacted with computers, making them accessible and intuitive for everyday consumers. In this section, we will explore the key contributions and impact of Apple on home computing.

Graphic User Interface (GUI) and the Macintosh

One of Apple's major contributions to home computing was the introduction of the graphical user interface (GUI) with the release of the Macintosh in 1984. Unlike the text-based interfaces of previous computers, the Macintosh allowed users to interact with the computer using icons, windows, and a mouse pointer. This shift in interface design made computers more visually appealing and easier to use for non-technical users.

The Macintosh also brought about the concept of "WYSIWYG" (What You See Is What You Get) in word processing and desktop publishing. Apple's software, such as MacWrite and MacPaint, allowed users to see on the screen exactly what would be printed, making document creation and editing much more user-friendly.

Apple's Impact on Home Computing

Apple's innovative products and design philosophy had a significant impact on the home computing industry. Here are some key aspects of their influence:

1. **User-Friendly Design:** Apple's focus on user experience and design aesthetics made computing more accessible and attractive to a wider audience. The sleek and intuitive design of Apple products, such as the iMac, MacBook, and iPhone, set a new standard in the industry.

2. **Multimedia Capabilities:** Apple's emphasis on multimedia capabilities played a major role in shaping the home computing landscape. The introduction of software like iTunes, iMovie, and GarageBand provided users with seamless ways to manage their music, create videos, and produce music, fostering a new era of digital content creation.

3. **Integration of Hardware and Software:** Unlike many competitors, Apple integrated hardware and software seamlessly, ensuring a high level of compatibility and user

experience. By controlling both the hardware and software aspects, Apple delivered a more cohesive and reliable computing experience to its customers.

4. **iPod and iTunes:** Apple's introduction of the iPod in 2001 brought portable digital music players into the mainstream. Combined with iTunes, Apple's music management software, the iPod revolutionized the way people listened to and purchased music, paving the way for the digital music industry we know today.

5. **iPhone and the App Store:** The launch of the iPhone in 2007 completely transformed the concept of a mobile phone. With the App Store, Apple created a platform for developers to create and distribute a wide variety of applications, revolutionizing the way we communicate, work, and entertain ourselves on our phones.

6. **Apple Ecosystem:** Apple's interconnectivity between devices and services, known as the Apple ecosystem, has created a seamless and integrated experience for users. Features like iCloud, Handoff, and Continuity allow devices to sync and communicate effortlessly, adding convenience and productivity for home computing.

Overall, Apple's impact on home computing has been significant and enduring. Through their focus on user-friendly design, multimedia capabilities, hardware-software integration, and the creation of iconic products like the Macintosh, iPod, and iPhone, Apple has shaped the way we interact with technology in our homes.

Resources

If you are interested in learning more about Apple's impact on home computing, the following resources are recommended:

- *The Steve Jobs Way: iLeadership for a New Generation* by Jay Elliot and William L. Simon.
- *Becoming Steve Jobs: The Evolution of a Reckless Upstart into a Visionary Leader* by Brent Schlender and Rick Tetzeli.
- *Insanely Great: The Life and Times of Macintosh, the Computer that Changed Everything* by Steven Levy.
- *Jony Ive: The Genius Behind Apple's Greatest Products* by Leander Kahney.

These books provide valuable insights into the history, ideology, and impact of Apple in the world of home computing.

Trick: Optimizing Mac Performance

If you are a Mac user and want to optimize the performance of your device, try resetting the System Management Controller (SMC). This can help with issues like slow performance, decreased battery life, and unusual behavior. To reset the SMC on desktop Macs, shut down your Mac, unplug the power cord, wait for 15 seconds, and then plug it back in and start your Mac. For MacBook models with a non-removable battery, shut down your Mac, press Shift-Control-Option on the left side of the keyboard, and then press the power button simultaneously. Release all keys and the power button, then press the power button to turn on your Mac.

Exercise

Think about a technological innovation or product that has had a significant impact on home computing in the past decade. Write a short essay explaining how it has transformed the way people interact with technology at home, considering its design, functionality, and the broader implications it has had on society.

Apple's Expanding Product Line

Throughout its history, Apple Inc. has been at the forefront of innovation in the world of technology. From its humble beginnings with the Apple I computer, the company has continuously expanded its product line, introducing groundbreaking devices that have revolutionized the consumer electronics industry. This section will explore the key milestones in Apple's product development, highlighting the significant contributions made by the company.

The Macintosh

The introduction of the Macintosh in 1984 marked a significant turning point for Apple. The Macintosh, with its revolutionary graphical user interface (GUI), brought computing to the masses and set the stage for Apple's future success. The GUI, developed by Xerox PARC and refined by Apple, replaced the traditional text-based command line interface with a visually appealing and intuitive system of icons, windows, and menus. This innovation made computers more accessible and user-friendly than ever before.

With the success of the Macintosh, Apple began to expand its product line to cater to different types of users. The Macintosh Plus, released in 1986, featured a larger memory capacity and expanded storage options, making it popular with professionals and creative individuals. The Macintosh SE and Macintosh II series, introduced in the late 1980s and early 1990s, offered enhanced performance and graphical capabilities, targeting the high-end market.

iPod and iTunes

In 2001, Apple revolutionized the music industry with the introduction of the iPod. The iPod, a portable digital music player, allowed users to carry their entire music library in their pocket. It featured a simple and elegant design, with a click wheel interface that made navigation effortless. The integration of iTunes, Apple's digital music software, provided a seamless way to manage and organize music, as well as purchase songs from the iTunes Store.

The success of the iPod and iTunes ecosystem paved the way for Apple's expansion into the realm of mobile devices. Building upon the success of the iPod, Apple introduced the iPhone in 2007. The iPhone combined the features of a mobile phone, an iPod, and an Internet communication device into a single device, revolutionizing the smartphone industry. With its sleek design, multi-touch display, and intuitive user interface, the iPhone quickly became a cultural phenomenon.

iPad and Apple Watch

Expanding its product line further, Apple introduced the iPad in 2010. The iPad offered a larger form factor than the iPhone, bridging the gap between smartphones and laptops. With its intuitive touch interface and a variety of apps optimized for the larger screen, the iPad revolutionized the tablet market. It became a popular device for content consumption, productivity, and creative tasks.

In 2015, Apple released the Apple Watch, marking its entry into the wearable technology market. The Apple Watch combined fitness tracking, communication, and app integration into a stylish and functional device. With its advanced sensors and health monitoring features, the Apple Watch has become a popular choice for fitness enthusiasts and individuals seeking a convenient way to track their health metrics.

Expanding Beyond Hardware

In addition to hardware products, Apple has also expanded its product line to include software and services. The introduction of iCloud in 2011 provided seamless integration and synchronization across Apple devices, allowing users to access their content from anywhere. Apple Music, launched in 2015, provided a streaming service that competed with other music streaming platforms.

Furthermore, Apple has ventured into the world of subscription services with the introduction of Apple TV+ and Apple Arcade. Apple TV+ offers original programming and content, while Apple Arcade provides a curated collection of games for users to enjoy on their Apple devices.

Conclusion

Apple's expanding product line has demonstrated its commitment to innovation and excellence in the field of technology. From the Macintosh to the iPhone, iPad, Apple Watch, and a range of software and services, Apple has continuously pushed boundaries and transformed the way we interact with technology. As Apple continues to evolve and introduce new products, it will undoubtedly shape the future of consumer electronics and maintain its position as a leader in the industry.

IBM PC: Bringing Computing to the Masses

DOS vs. Windows

In the early days of personal computing, one of the most significant battles was between DOS (Disk Operating System) and Windows. DOS was the dominant operating system in the

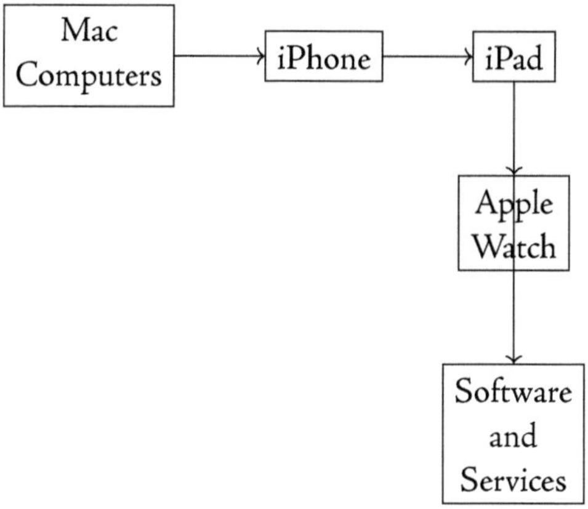

Figure 0.2: Apple's Expanding Product Line

1980s, and it played a crucial role in the emergence of the PC industry. However, with the introduction of Windows, a new era of computing began, transforming the way people interacted with computers. In this section, we will explore the key differences between DOS and Windows, their impact on the computing landscape, and how Windows eventually overshadowed DOS.

The Rise of DOS

DOS was developed by Microsoft in the early 1980s as an operating system for IBM's newly released personal computer, the IBM PC. It provided a command-line interface, allowing users to communicate with the computer through typed commands. At the time, the personal computer industry was in its infancy, and DOS played a critical role in popularizing computers for the masses.

The Limitations of DOS

While DOS was a significant milestone in personal computing, it had some limitations that hindered its usability and accessibility. Its command-line interface required users to have a technical understanding of computer commands, which made it challenging for non-technical users to operate. Additionally, DOS lacked multitasking capabilities, meaning only one program could run at a time. Moreover, DOS had no built-in graphical user interface (GUI), which made it less visually appealing and intuitive compared to modern-day operating systems.

The Birth of Windows

To address the drawbacks of DOS, Microsoft introduced Windows in 1985. Windows was an operating system that provided a graphical user interface, allowing users to interact with the computer using icons, menus, and windows. This introduced a more intuitive and user-friendly way of navigating and using computers.

DOS vs. Windows: User Experience

The key difference between DOS and Windows was the user experience. DOS relied on text-based commands, which required users to memorize specific commands and type them correctly to perform tasks. With Windows, users could perform actions by simply clicking on icons or selecting options from menus, making computing more accessible to a broader range of users.

DOS vs. Windows: Multitasking

Another significant difference between DOS and Windows was multitasking. DOS could only run one program at a time, requiring users to exit one program before launching another.

Windows introduced true multitasking, allowing users to run multiple programs simultaneously, improving productivity and efficiency.

DOS vs. Windows: Graphical User Interface

One of the most transformative aspects of Windows was its graphical user interface. With Windows, users could visually interact with their computers. Instead of typing commands, they could navigate through a series of menus and windows. This made computing more intuitive and visually appealing, revolutionizing the user experience.

The Dominance of Windows

Despite its initial popularity, DOS eventually lost its dominance to Windows. Windows provided a more user-friendly and visually appealing experience, attracting a broader user base. With each new version, Windows introduced new features and improvements that further solidified its position as the leading operating system.

The Legacy of DOS

Although DOS eventually faded into obscurity, its legacy lives on. Many software applications and games were developed for DOS, and some enthusiasts still enjoy running DOS-based programs on emulators or virtual machines. Furthermore, DOS played a crucial role in setting the foundation for the evolution of operating systems, paving the way for user-friendly interfaces and multitasking capabilities.

Conclusion

The transition from DOS to Windows marked a paradigm shift in personal computing. Windows introduced a user-friendly graphical interface and multitasking capabilities, revolutionizing the way people interacted with computers. While DOS laid the foundation for the PC industry, it was Windows that ultimately democratized computing and made it accessible to a broader audience.

IBM-Compatible PCs and Clones

In the early days of personal computing, IBM played a central role in shaping the industry with its introduction of the IBM Personal Computer (PC) in 1981. The IBM PC, along with its operating system, MS-DOS, quickly became the standard for business computing. However, IBM's decision to use off-the-shelf components and allow other companies to produce IBM-compatible computers opened up a new era of competition and innovation.

The Rise of Clones

The release of the IBM PC created an opportunity for other companies to enter the market and produce their own versions of the IBM-compatible computer. These computers, known as clones, were designed to be compatible with IBM's hardware and software, allowing users to run the same software on non-IBM machines.

One of the key factors that led to the rise of clones was IBM's decision to use an open architecture for the IBM PC. This meant that IBM published detailed technical specifications and allowed other companies to create compatible hardware. This open architecture allowed cloning companies to reverse-engineer the IBM PC and produce their own compatible machines.

Cloning companies such as Compaq, Dell, and Gateway quickly emerged and gained popularity. These companies offered cheaper alternatives to the IBM PC, often with better performance and additional features. As a result, IBM-compatible clones started to dominate the personal computer market, eventually surpassing IBM's own sales.

Compatibility Challenges

While IBM-compatible clones offered users a more affordable option, there were challenges associated with compatibility. IBM had a strong hold on the market and constantly updated its machines, introducing new features and hardware enhancements.

Cloning companies had to navigate the challenge of keeping up with IBM's hardware and software changes. They had to reverse-engineer each new generation of IBM machines to ensure compatibility with existing software. This created a race to match IBM's innovation while also maintaining compatibility, which was not always an easy task.

The Battle of Operating Systems

Another significant development in the IBM-compatible PC market was the emergence of alternative operating systems to IBM's MS-DOS. While MS-DOS remained the dominant operating system for IBM-compatible computers, other operating systems such as Unix and OS/2 gained traction among certain user groups.

Unix, originally developed by AT&T Bell Labs, gained popularity among the academic and scientific communities. It provided a more powerful and flexible operating system compared to MS-DOS, allowing users to run multiple tasks simultaneously.

OS/2, developed jointly by IBM and Microsoft, was positioned as the successor to MS-DOS. It offered significant improvements in terms of multitasking, stability, and graphical user interface. However, despite its potential, OS/2 faced challenges in gaining widespread adoption due to compatibility issues and the dominance of MS-DOS.

Legacy and Impact

The era of IBM-compatible PCs and clones had a profound impact on the personal computer industry. It brought about competition and innovation, driving down prices and expanding the market for personal computers. The open architecture of the IBM PC paved the way for a diverse ecosystem of hardware and software manufacturers.

The compatibility challenges faced by cloning companies also contributed to the development of industry standards. As companies strived to maintain compatibility with IBM's hardware and software, they developed industry standards such as the Extended Industry Standard Architecture (EISA), which provided a standardized expansion bus for PCs.

Furthermore, the battle of operating systems in the IBM-compatible PC market helped shape the future of computing. MS-DOS, despite its limitations, laid the foundation for the dominance of Microsoft's Windows operating system in the years to come.

Conclusion

The rise of IBM-compatible PCs and clones revolutionized the personal computer industry. Cloning companies capitalized on IBM's open architecture to offer cheaper and more innovative alternatives to the IBM PC. This era of competition and innovation laid the foundation for the diverse and dynamic personal computer market we see today.

Networking and the Internet

ARPANET: The Precursor to the Internet

Tim Berners-Lee's World Wide Web

Browser Wars: Netscape vs. Internet Explorer

The browser wars of the late 1990s was a defining moment in the history of computing and the internet. It was a battle between Netscape Navigator and Internet Explorer that would shape the future of web browsing and set the stage for the dominance of Microsoft in the browser market. In this section, we will delve into the origins of the browser wars, the key players involved, the strategies they employed, and the lasting impact on the world wide web.

Origins of the Browser Wars

In the early days of the internet, there was a lack of standardization for web browsing. Various browsers, such as Mosaic and Lynx, offered different capabilities and supported different features. However, in 1994, Netscape Communications Corporation released Netscape Navigator, a groundbreaking browser that introduced many features that we take for granted today, including images, tables, and frames. This marked the beginning of a new era in web browsing.

Netscape Navigator quickly gained popularity and became the dominant browser in the market. By 1995, it held a staggering 90

Microsoft Enters the Fray

Recognizing the potential of the internet, Microsoft saw an opportunity to integrate web browsing directly into its Windows operating system. In 1995, they released Internet Explorer as an add-on to Windows 95. This move was met with criticism as many believed it was an attempt by Microsoft to dominate the browser market by leveraging its monopoly in the operating system space.

Over the next few years, Netscape and Microsoft engaged in fierce competition to win the hearts and minds of internet users. Both companies constantly released new versions of their browsers, each offering improved features and performance. This led to a flurry of innovation and rapid progression in web technologies.

Feature Wars and Standards

One of the key battlegrounds in the browser wars was support for web standards. Netscape and Microsoft each had their own proprietary technologies, such as Netscape's JavaScript and Microsoft's ActiveX, that they used to differentiate their browsers. This led to websites being designed specifically for one browser, creating compatibility issues for users and developers alike.

To address these issues, the World Wide Web Consortium (W3C) was established in 1994 to develop and promote open standards for the web. The W3C's standards, such as HTML,

CSS, and JavaScript, aimed to ensure that websites would work across different browsers and platforms.

Despite the efforts of the W3C, the browser wars continued to be fueled by the introduction of new features and technologies. This led to a fragmentation of the web, with websites often requiring specific browsers or versions to be properly displayed.

The Browser War Ends

The browser wars reached a turning point in the early 2000s when Microsoft started bundling Internet Explorer with Windows, giving it an unfair advantage over Netscape Navigator. As a result, Netscape's market share began to decline rapidly.

In 1998, Netscape took a bold step by releasing the source code of its browser, resulting in the creation of the open-source Mozilla project. This marked the birth of the Mozilla Firefox browser, which would become a major player in the browser market in the years to come.

Despite the increasing competition, Microsoft maintained its dominance in the browser market for several years. However, in 2004, a new challenger emerged in the form of Mozilla Firefox. Firefox gained popularity for its focus on standards compliance, performance, and security.

The browser wars eventually came to an end in the late 2000s as new contenders, such as Google Chrome and Apple Safari, entered the market. These browsers offered improved performance, security, and a better user experience. Today, Google Chrome is the most widely used browser, with a market share of over 60

Legacy of the Browser Wars

The browser wars had a lasting impact on the world wide web. One of the most significant outcomes was the increased focus on web standards and compatibility. The need for web developers to ensure their websites work across different browsers led to a more unified and standardized web.

Another lasting legacy is the rise of open-source browsers. Mozilla Firefox, born from the ashes of Netscape, demonstrated the power of open-source development and community collaboration. It paved the way for the success of other open-source projects and a more diverse browser ecosystem.

The browser wars also shaped the strategies and tactics used by companies in the tech industry. The battle between Netscape and Microsoft highlighted the importance of establishing dominance in key markets and leveraging one's existing position to gain a competitive advantage.

Conclusion

The browser wars between Netscape Navigator and Internet Explorer forever transformed the landscape of web browsing. It was a clash of titans that propelled technological innovation and led to a more standardized web experience. While the browser wars may be a thing of the past, their impact continues to shape the way we browse the internet today.

Rise of E-Commerce

E-commerce, or electronic commerce, refers to the buying and selling of goods and services over the internet. It has revolutionized the way we shop and conduct business, providing convenience, accessibility, and global reach. In this section, we will explore the growth and impact of e-commerce, the key players in the industry, and the factors that have contributed to its success.

The Emergence of E-Commerce

The roots of e-commerce can be traced back to the early days of the internet. In the 1990s, as the World Wide Web became more accessible to the general public, businesses started exploring the potential of online sales. The rise of e-commerce was fueled by several factors:

- **Internet Penetration:** As internet connectivity became more widespread, more people gained access to online platforms, creating a larger customer base for e-commerce businesses.

- **Advancements in Technology:** The development of secure online payment systems, such as encrypted transactions and digital wallets, made it safer and more convenient for customers to make purchases online.

- **Changing Consumer Behavior:** Consumers embraced the convenience of shopping from the comfort of their homes and the ability to compare prices and reviews online before making a purchase decision.

Major Players in E-Commerce

Several major players have shaped the e-commerce landscape and contributed to its growth. These players include:

- **Amazon:** Founded by Jeff Bezos in 1994, Amazon started as an online bookstore and rapidly expanded to become the world's largest e-commerce platform. With its wide range of products, competitive pricing, and efficient delivery system, Amazon has set the standard for e-commerce excellence.
- **Alibaba:** Founded by Jack Ma in 1999, Alibaba is a Chinese e-commerce conglomerate that operates various platforms, including Taobao, Tmall, and AliExpress. Alibaba has played a key role in connecting businesses and consumers around the world, particularly in the Chinese market.
- **eBay:** Founded in 1995, eBay pioneered the concept of online auctions. It provided a platform for individuals and businesses to buy and sell a wide range of products in an auction-style format. While eBay's prominence has diminished over time, it remains an important player in the e-commerce industry.
- **Walmart:** As one of the largest retail corporations in the world, Walmart has embraced e-commerce to reach a wider customer base. By offering online shopping options and integrating e-commerce into its brick-and-mortar stores, Walmart has successfully adapted to the changing retail landscape.

The Impact of E-Commerce

The rise of e-commerce has had a profound impact on various aspects of our lives, including:

- **Convenience:** E-commerce has made shopping more convenient than ever before. Customers can browse and purchase products from anywhere at any time, eliminating the need to visit physical stores. This has particularly benefited people with limited mobility, those living in remote areas, and busy individuals.
- **Global Reach:** E-commerce has transcended geographical boundaries, allowing businesses to reach customers worldwide. This has opened up new market opportunities for small businesses and enabled them to compete on a global scale.
- **Price Comparison and Reviews:** Online shopping enables customers to compare prices, read reviews, and make informed purchase decisions. This transparency and accessibility of information have empowered consumers and facilitated fair competition between businesses.
- **Job Creation:** The growth of e-commerce has created numerous job opportunities, both directly and indirectly. From warehouse employees and delivery personnel to web developers and digital marketers, e-commerce has contributed to job growth across various industries.

Challenges and Concerns

While e-commerce has brought numerous benefits, it also presents challenges and concerns that need to be addressed:

- **Security and Privacy:** With the increasing number of online transactions, the risk of data breaches and identity theft has become a major concern. E-commerce platforms must prioritize security measures to protect customer information and build trust.

- **Logistics and Fulfillment:** Delivering products to customers in a timely and efficient manner is crucial for e-commerce success. It requires robust logistics networks, effective inventory management, and partnerships with reliable shipping carriers.
- **Competition and Market Saturation:** The e-commerce industry is highly competitive, with numerous businesses vying for customers' attention and loyalty. Achieving differentiation and standing out from the crowd can be challenging, especially for smaller businesses.
- **Sustainability and Environmental Impact:** The growing volume of e-commerce transactions has raised concerns about its environmental impact, such as packaging waste and carbon emissions from transportation. Balancing the convenience of online shopping with sustainable practices is a pressing issue.

Future Trends and Opportunities

The future of e-commerce holds exciting possibilities. Here are some emerging trends and opportunities to watch for:

- **Mobile Commerce:** With the increasing use of smartphones and mobile devices, mobile commerce (m-commerce) is set to grow. Businesses must optimize their online platforms for mobile devices and provide seamless shopping experiences across multiple channels.
- **Personalization and AI:** Artificial intelligence (AI) technologies have the potential to personalize the e-commerce experience further. From personalized product recommendations to chatbots providing customer support, AI can enhance customer engagement and satisfaction.

- **Omnichannel Retail:** Integrating online and offline channels is gaining importance in the e-commerce industry. Customers expect a seamless experience across different touchpoints, combining the convenience of online shopping with the tactile experience of physical stores.

- **Sustainability and Green Practices:** E-commerce businesses are increasingly adopting sustainable practices to reduce their environmental footprint. This includes using eco-friendly packaging materials, optimizing transportation routes, and promoting ethical sourcing.

Conclusion

The rise of e-commerce has transformed the way we buy and sell products, enabling convenience, global reach, and new business opportunities. As the industry continues to evolve, addressing challenges such as security and sustainability while embracing emerging trends will be key to its future success. In the next section, we will explore the protocols and standards that underpin the functioning of the internet, making e-commerce possible.

Dot-Com Bubble: Boom and Bust

The Dot-Com Bubble, also known as the Internet Bubble, was a period of rapid growth and excessive speculation in the stock prices of internet-based companies in the late 1990s and early 2000s. It was characterized by the emergence of numerous dot-com companies, fueled by the increasing popularity of the internet and the belief that the internet would revolutionize business and society.

Background

The Dot-Com Bubble can be traced back to the early days of the internet when it was primarily used for academic and military purposes. As the internet became more accessible to the general public, entrepreneurs saw an opportunity to build new companies that leveraged the power of the internet.

Investors were excited about the potential of these companies to disrupt traditional industries and create significant wealth. Many internet companies went public, often with little or no profits, and experienced dramatic increases in stock prices. This led to a frenzy of buying, as investors wanted to get in on the action and didn't want to miss out on the next big thing.

Boom

During the dot-com boom, internet stocks were in high demand, with investors rushing to invest in companies that promised exponential growth in a short period. The stock prices of these companies skyrocketed, creating substantial paper wealth for investors and attracting new investors hoping to profit from the trend.

Investors were attracted to the potential of internet companies to disrupt traditional industries and create new business models. Companies like Amazon, eBay, and Yahoo were seen as pioneers in e-commerce and online advertising, and their stock prices soared.

Venture capitalists flooded the market with money, fueling the growth of startups and providing funding for new ideas. The perception was that the internet had fundamentally changed the rules of business, and any company with an online presence could achieve enormous success.

Bust

The excessive speculation and unrealistic valuations of internet companies eventually led to the burst of the dot-com bubble. As more companies went public, investors started to realize that many of these companies had little or no revenue, and their business models were unsustainable.

Market sentiment shifted, and investors became more cautious. They started to question the viability of the business models of these internet companies and their ability to generate profits in the long term.

In early 2000, the stock market started to decline, and many dot-com stocks plummeted in value. This triggered a wave of panic selling, as investors tried to get out before prices fell further. Companies that were once considered high-flying tech darlings saw their stock prices collapse, leading to significant losses for investors.

The bursting of the dot-com bubble had far-reaching consequences. Many internet companies went out of business, leading to massive job losses and a decline in investor confidence. The overall stock market also suffered, with the Nasdaq Composite Index, which was heavily weighted towards technology stocks, losing more than 75

Lessons Learned

The dot-com bubble and its subsequent burst taught valuable lessons about investing and the nature of technology-driven markets.

Firstly, it highlighted the importance of fundamental analysis and rational valuation when investing in stocks. Many investors at the time were caught up in the hype and invested based on the expectation of future price appreciation rather than the underlying business fundamentals.

Secondly, it demonstrated the importance of diversification in an investment portfolio. Those investors who had a well-diversified portfolio that included assets beyond tech stocks were better able to weather the storm of the dot-com burst.

Lastly, it showed that technology-driven markets are prone to volatility and speculative excesses. While the internet has indeed revolutionized many industries, not all internet companies were able to deliver on their promises of profitability and growth.

Current Implications

The dot-com bubble has had a lasting impact on the business and investment landscape. It has made investors more cautious when it comes to valuing technology stocks and has resulted in a greater emphasis on profitability and sustainable business models.

Furthermore, it has shaped the way startups are funded and evaluated. Venture capitalists and angel investors are now more focused on the viability and scalability of a business rather than simply the potential of its technology.

The dot-com bubble also serves as a reminder of the risks associated with speculative investment strategies and the dangers of ignoring traditional investing principles. It emphasizes the importance of conducting thorough due diligence and not getting caught up in market hype.

While the burst of the dot-com bubble led to a temporary setback for the technology industry, it ultimately paved the way for a more mature and sustainable tech sector that continues to drive innovation and economic growth today.

Conclusion

The Dot-Com Bubble was a period of excessive speculation and skyrocketing stock prices in internet-based companies. It eventually burst, leading to significant losses for investors and a decline in investor confidence.

The dot-com boom and bust taught valuable lessons about investing and the nature of technology-driven markets. It emphasized the importance of fundamental analysis, diversification, and rational valuation. It also shaped the way startups are funded and evaluated, with a greater emphasis on viable business models.

While the burst of the dot-com bubble had a temporary setback for the technology industry, it ultimately led to a more mature and sustainable tech sector that continues to drive innovation and economic growth.

Internet Protocols and Standards

TCP/IP and the Foundation of Internet Communication

The Internet has become an integral part of our daily lives, allowing us to communicate, share information, and access resources from around the world. At the heart of the Internet's success is the TCP/IP protocol suite, which provides a robust and reliable communication framework. In this section, we will explore the principles and mechanisms behind TCP/IP and how it forms the foundation of Internet communication.

Overview of TCP/IP

TCP/IP, which stands for Transmission Control Protocol/Internet Protocol, is a set of communication protocols that define how computers and other devices exchange data over the Internet. Developed in the 1970s and 1980s, TCP/IP has become the de facto standard for network communication.

The TCP/IP protocol suite consists of several protocols that work together to ensure the reliable delivery of data. The two main protocols in TCP/IP are TCP and IP. TCP provides a connection-oriented service, ensuring that data is delivered in the correct order and without errors. IP, on the other hand, is responsible for addressing and routing packets across the Internet.

IP Addressing

One of the key components of the TCP/IP protocol suite is the IP addressing scheme. An IP address is a unique identifier assigned to each device on a network. It consists of four numbers, separated by periods, with each number ranging from 0 to 255 (e.g., 192.168.0.1).

IP addresses are divided into two types: IPv4 and IPv6. IPv4 addresses, which are the most commonly used, are 32 bits long and have a limited address space. With the increasing number of devices connected to the Internet, the need for more IP addresses led to the development of IPv6, which uses 128-bit addresses and provides a virtually unlimited address space.

Packet Switching

TCP/IP relies on packet switching to transmit data over the Internet. Packet switching breaks data into smaller units called packets and sends them individually over the network. This allows for more efficient use of network resources and better reliability.

When data is sent over the Internet, it is divided into packets at the sender's end. Each packet contains a portion of the original data, as well as the necessary addressing information. These packets are then transmitted independently over the network and reassembled at the receiver's end to reconstruct the original data.

TCP: Reliable Data Delivery

TCP (Transmission Control Protocol) is responsible for the reliable delivery of data over the Internet. It ensures that data is delivered in the correct order, without errors, and with flow control to prevent overload.

To achieve reliable data delivery, TCP uses several mechanisms. It establishes a connection between the sender and receiver before data transfer begins, using a three-way handshake. This ensures that both parties are ready to exchange data.

TCP also uses sequence numbers to order the packets and acknowledgments to acknowledge the receipt of packets. If a packet is lost or damaged during transmission, TCP will retransmit it to ensure its delivery. Additionally, TCP implements congestion control algorithms to regulate the flow of data and prevent network congestion.

IP: Addressing and Routing

While TCP is responsible for data delivery, IP (Internet Protocol) handles addressing and routing. IP provides a unique IP address to each device connected to the Internet and ensures that packets are correctly routed to their destination.

When a packet is sent over the Internet, it contains both the source and destination IP addresses. Routers, which are specialized devices that forward packets between networks, use the destination IP address to determine the best path for the packet to reach its destination. This process is known as routing.

IP routing relies on routing tables, which contain information about the network topology and the available paths for packet transmission. Routers use these tables to make intelligent decisions about packet forwarding, ensuring efficient and reliable delivery.

DNS: Mapping IP Addresses to Domain Names

The Domain Name System (DNS) is an integral part of TCP/IP, as it allows us to use domain names (such as www.example.com) instead of IP addresses to access resources on the Internet. DNS acts as a distributed directory service, translating domain names into IP addresses.

When we enter a domain name into a web browser, the browser first sends a DNS query to a DNS server to obtain the corresponding IP address. The DNS server then replies with the IP address, allowing the browser to establish a connection to the desired resource.

DNS operates in a hierarchical structure, with multiple levels of DNS servers. At the top of the hierarchy are the root DNS servers, which have information about the top-level domains (e.g., .com, .org). Below the root servers are the authoritative DNS servers, which hold the specific DNS records for individual domains.

Security Considerations

Ensuring the security of Internet communication is of utmost importance. TCP/IP incorporates various security measures to protect against unauthorized access, data tampering, and other security threats.

The most commonly used security protocol in TCP/IP is the Secure Socket Layer (SSL) or its successor, Transport Layer Security (TLS). These protocols provide encryption and authentication mechanisms to secure data transmitted over the network. By encrypting the data, SSL/TLS prevents eavesdropping and ensures data integrity.

Another important aspect of security in TCP/IP is the use of firewalls and routers with advanced security features. Firewalls act as a barrier between a trusted internal network and the

Internet, inspecting and filtering network traffic to prevent unauthorized access. Routers can also be configured to implement access control and filtering rules to protect the network.

Conclusion

TCP/IP is the backbone of the Internet, providing a robust and reliable communication framework. Its protocols, such as TCP, IP, and DNS, ensure the delivery of data, addressing, and routing, and the translation of domain names to IP addresses. By understanding the principles behind TCP/IP, we gain insights into how the Internet works and how it has revolutionized communication and the exchange of information in our modern society.

Resources

Here are some resources for further reading on TCP/IP and Internet communication:

- Comer, D. E. (2014). *Internetworking with TCP/IP, Vol. 1: Principles, Protocols, and Architecture.*

- Tanenbaum, A. S., Wetherall, D. J., & Steen, M. V. (2011). *Computer Networks.*

- Kurose, J. F., & Ross, K. W. (2017). *Computer Networking: A Top-Down Approach.*

These books provide in-depth explanations of networking principles and TCP/IP protocols, making them valuable resources for further exploration.

HTTP/HTTPS: The Language of the Web

HTTP (Hypertext Transfer Protocol) and HTTPS (Hypertext Transfer Protocol Secure) are the two key protocols that enable communication between clients (such as web browsers) and servers on the World Wide Web. They define the rules and format for exchanging data, enabling the retrieval and display of websites, multimedia content, and other resources. In this section, we will explore the concepts behind these protocols, their differences, and their importance in establishing secure communication over the internet.

Introduction to HTTP

HTTP is the foundation of data communication on the web. It is a stateless protocol, which means that each request and response stands on its own without any memory of previous interactions. When a client, such as a web browser, wants to retrieve a resource from a server, it sends an HTTP request containing specific instructions and headers to the server. The server then responds with an HTTP response, which includes the requested resource or an error message.

The structure of an HTTP request typically consists of a request line, headers, and an optional message body. The request line contains the HTTP method (such as GET, POST, or PUT) along with the URL of the resource. The headers provide additional information about the request, such as the type of data the client accepts or the format of the response expected. The message body, if present, carries additional data, such as form inputs or file attachments.

Here is an example of an HTTP request:

```
GET /index.html HTTP/1.1
Host: www.example\index{example}.com\index{com}
Accept: text/html
```

In this example, the client is requesting the "index.html" file from the "www.example.com" server and specifies that it accepts HTML content.

HTTP Response Codes

HTTP responses contain a status line, headers, and an optional message body. The status line includes a numeric status code and a textual status message that indicates whether the request was successful or encountered an error.

Some commonly encountered HTTP response codes include:

- **200 OK:** The request was successful, and the requested resource is included in the response.
- **404 Not Found:** The requested resource could not be found on the server.
- **301 Moved Permanently:** The requested resource has been permanently moved to a new URL.
- **500 Internal Server Error:** The server encountered an error while processing the request.

These status codes help the client understand the outcome of the request and take appropriate actions.

Introduction to HTTPS

While HTTP allows for the transmission of data over the internet, it lacks security measures to protect sensitive information from eavesdropping or tampering. This is where HTTPS comes in. HTTPS encrypts the data exchanged between the client and server using encryption protocols, typically SSL (Secure Sockets Layer) or its successor, TLS (Transport Layer Security).

HTTPS operates on top of HTTP, using the same request-response structure. However, the communication is encrypted and secured, ensuring the confidentiality and integrity of the transmitted data.

To establish an HTTPS connection, the client and server perform a process known as the SSL/TLS handshake. During this handshake, the client and server exchange digital certificates to prove their identities, negotiate encryption protocols, and agree on a shared secret key for symmetric encryption.

Benefits of HTTPS

The use of HTTPS provides several important benefits for both website owners and users:

- **Data Encryption:** HTTPS ensures that the data exchanged between the client and server is encrypted, preventing unauthorized access and eavesdropping.
- **Data Integrity:** HTTPS protects the integrity of the data, ensuring that it cannot be modified or tampered with during transmission.
- **Authentication:** By using digital certificates, HTTPS enables the client to authenticate the identity of the server, establishing trust and preventing impersonation attacks.
- **SEO Advantage:** Search engines prioritize websites using HTTPS, as it provides a safer browsing experience for users.

Using HTTPS to Secure Web Applications

To secure web applications, website owners need to configure their servers to use HTTPS. This involves obtaining an SSL/TLS certificate from a trusted certificate authority and configuring the server to enable secure connections over HTTPS. Additionally, website owners must ensure that all resources (such as images, scripts, and stylesheets) are also served via HTTPS to prevent mixed-content warnings.

Web browsers play a crucial role in HTTPS adoption by displaying a padlock icon in the address bar to indicate a secure connection and warning users when a website does not have a valid SSL/TLS certificate.

Certification Authorities and Public Key Infrastructure

SSL/TLS certificates used for HTTPS are issued by certification authorities (CAs) who vouch for the authenticity of the certificate holder's identity. CAs are trusted entities that follow strict procedures for verifying the identity of the certificate applicant. This verification process helps establish trust in the certificate and the corresponding HTTPS connection.

Public key infrastructure (PKI) is a framework that enables the secure exchange of information in a networked environment. PKI relies on the use of digital certificates, public and private keys, and trusted third-party CAs to ensure the confidentiality, integrity, and authenticity of data exchanged between entities.

HTTP/2 and Beyond

While HTTP has been the backbone of web communication for decades, newer versions have been developed to address its limitations and enhance performance. One significant enhancement is HTTP/2, which introduces features such as multiplexing, header compression, and server push. These improvements aim to reduce latency, improve page load times, and optimize the use of network resources.

Looking ahead, the future of web communication may involve emerging protocols, such as QUIC (Quick UDP Internet

Connections), which aims to further improve performance and security by using the User Datagram Protocol (UDP).

Conclusion

HTTP and HTTPS are the fundamental protocols that enable communication on the web. Understanding their structure, purpose, and differences is essential for anyone involved in web development or using the internet. By adopting HTTPS and adhering to secure web practices, we can protect sensitive information, secure online transactions, and ensure a safer browsing experience for all users.

Software Revolution

Unix and Open Source Movement

Microsoft Windows

Linux: The Open Source Challenger

GNU Project and Free Software Foundation

In the world of computing, software plays a crucial role in enabling the functionality and operation of computer systems. The traditional model of software development involves closed-source proprietary software, where the source code is not available to users. However, in the late 1970s, the emergence of the GNU Project and the Free Software Foundation (FSF) challenged this model by advocating for the principles of free and open-source software (FOSS). This subsection explores the history, purpose, and impact of the GNU Project and the FSF in promoting the ideals of free software.

History of the GNU Project

The GNU Project was launched in 1983 by Richard Stallman, a renowned computer scientist and software freedom advocate. The acronym GNU stands for "GNU's Not Unix," reflecting the project's goal of creating a free and open-source operating system compatible with the Unix operating system. Stallman envisioned a software ecosystem that would allow users the freedom to run, study, modify, and distribute software according to their needs.

The GNU Project aimed to develop a complete Unix-like operating system composed entirely of free software. However, one critical component was missing: the kernel. To address this gap, Stallman founded the Free Software Foundation in 1985. The FSF is a non-profit organization dedicated to promoting and preserving software freedom.

Goals and Principles of the GNU Project and the FSF

The GNU Project and the FSF advocate for four essential freedoms for computer users:

1. The freedom to run the software for any purpose.
2. The freedom to study and modify the source code to suit individual needs.
3. The freedom to distribute copies to help others.
4. The freedom to distribute modified versions of the software.

These four freedoms form the foundation of the free software movement. They ensure that users have full control of the software they use, enabling them to customize and share it with others. By granting these freedoms, the GNU Project and the FSF promote collaboration, innovation, and user empowerment.

To protect these principles, the FSF developed the GNU General Public License (GPL), a widely used license for free software. The GPL ensures that any derivative work of free software remains free and openly available to all users. This copyleft provision prevents the appropriation of free software by proprietary software companies, ensuring its continual open-source nature.

Impact of the GNU Project and the FSF

The GNU Project and the FSF have had a profound impact on the field of computer science and the broader software industry. Their advocacy for free software has created a vibrant ecosystem of open-source projects and communities. Some notable achievements include:

- The GNU/Linux Operating System: The GNU Project's collaboration with Linus Torvalds, who developed the Linux kernel, led to the creation of the GNU/Linux operating system. Today, GNU/Linux distributions such as Ubuntu, Fedora, and Debian power numerous devices, from personal computers to servers.

- Open Source Software Movement: The free software philosophy promoted by the GNU Project and the FSF inspired the broader open-source software movement. This movement emphasizes collaboration, transparency, and community-driven development. Many successful open-source projects, such as the Apache web server, the Python programming language, and the MySQL database management system, owe their existence to these principles.

- Free Software Tools: Through the contributions of the GNU Project and the FSF, a vast array of free software tools have been developed. These tools, including the GNU Compiler Collection (GCC), the GNU Debugger (GDB), and the GNU Emacs text editor, have become essential components in the arsenal of developers worldwide.

- Social Impact: The free software movement championed by the GNU Project and the FSF has a broader social impact. By promoting the idea of software freedom, they highlighted the importance of user rights, privacy, and equal access to technology. This perspective challenges the monopoly of proprietary software companies and encourages a more democratic and inclusive approach to technology development and usage.

Challenges and Controversies

While the GNU Project and the FSF have made significant strides in promoting free software, they have faced challenges and controversies along the way. Some of these include:

- Compatibility and Fragmentation: The GNU/Linux operating system, born out of the collaboration between the GNU Project and the Linux kernel, faces challenges of compatibility and fragmentation. Different distributions, package managers, and software repositories can lead to inconsistencies and complexities for users.

- Corporate Influence: As free software gained prominence, companies started embracing open-source principles to varying degrees. Some companies, such as Red Hat, embraced the collaborative ethos of free software, while others used it as a marketing strategy to maintain control over their proprietary products.

- License Compliance: Ensuring compliance with the GNU GPL and other free software licenses remains a challenge. Organizations sometimes fail to meet their obligations of releasing source code modifications or distributing software under compatible licenses, potentially limiting the impact and freedom of the software.

- User Adoption: Despite the availability of free software alternatives, proprietary software still dominates in many areas. The challenges of familiarity, availability of specialized proprietary software, and compatibility with standardized formats can hinder widespread user adoption.

Conclusion

The GNU Project and the Free Software Foundation have played a crucial role in advocating for the principles of free and open-source software. Their work has transformed the software landscape and empowered users by promoting software freedom, collaboration, and transparency. The ongoing efforts of the GNU Project and the FSF continue to shape the future of computing, ensuring that software remains a shared resource for the benefit of all.

Mobile Computing

Evolution of Mobile Devices

Early Mobile Phones

In this section, we will explore the origins and development of early mobile phones. These early devices laid the foundation for the revolutionary communication devices we use today. We will delve into the technologies, design principles, and significant milestones that shaped the evolution of mobile phones.

The Birth of Mobile Telephony

Mobile telephony was born out of the need for wireless communication, enabling people to communicate while on the move. The concept of a mobile phone can be traced back to the early 20th century when researchers and inventors began exploring the possibility of wireless communication.

Predecessors to Mobile Phones

Before the emergence of mobile phones as we know them today, various wireless communication technologies paved the way for their development. Some notable predecessors include the telegraph, walkie-talkies, and car phones.

The telegraph, invented by Samuel Morse in the 1830s, was one of the earliest long-distance communication systems. It used electrical signals transmitted over wires to send messages. While not a mobile device in the traditional sense, it served as an inspiration for the development of wireless communication.

Walkie-talkies, initially used by the military during World War II, allowed users to communicate wirelessly over short distances. These handheld devices laid the groundwork for the development of portable and compact mobile phones.

Car phones were another precursor to modern mobile phones. Introduced in the mid-20th century, they were installed in vehicles and used radio waves for wireless communication. While they provided mobile communication, their size and limited range restricted their usability.

First Generation Mobile Phones

The first generation of mobile phones, commonly known as 1G, emerged in the 1980s. These devices were large, bulky, and primarily designed for voice calls. 1G phones relied on analog technology for wireless communication.

One of the earliest 1G mobile phones was the Motorola DynaTAC 8000X, which was commercially launched in 1983. This brick-shaped device weighed nearly two pounds and had a limited battery life. Despite its size and limitations, it was a breakthrough in mobile communication and served as a foundation for future devices.

Technological Advancements in Mobile Phones

Several technological advancements played a significant role in improving mobile phones and shaping their design. Here are a few key advancements:

- **Digital Cellular Networks:** The transition from analog to digital networks (2G) in the 1990s allowed for more efficient use of available frequencies, improved call quality, and the ability to send text messages.
- **SMS:** Short Message Service (SMS) was introduced in the late 1980s as a means of sending text messages between mobile phones. Initially, the character limit was limited to 160 characters, but it quickly became a popular form of communication.
- **Mobile Internet:** With the advent of 2.5G and 3G networks in the late 1990s and early 2000s, mobile phones gained the ability to access the internet. This opened up a world of possibilities for mobile phone users, allowing them to browse websites, send emails, and use web-based applications.
- **Multimedia Capabilities:** The integration of cameras, music players, and multimedia playback in mobile phones added entertainment and convenience to these devices. This trend continued with the introduction of video recording and playback capabilities.
- **Smartphones:** The introduction of smartphones marked a turning point in the evolution of mobile phones. These devices combined telephony with advanced computing capabilities, offering features such as touchscreen interfaces, app ecosystems, and seamless integration with online services.

Impact on Society

The proliferation of mobile phones has had a significant impact on society. Here are a few areas that have been influenced by mobile phones:

- **Communication:** Mobile phones have revolutionized communication by enabling instant and convenient connectivity. People can stay in touch with family, friends, and colleagues regardless of their location.
- **Economic Growth:** Mobile phones have played a crucial role in driving economic growth, particularly in developing countries. They have facilitated access to financial services, created job opportunities, and enhanced market connectivity.
- **Education:** Mobile phones have transformed education by providing access to educational content, online courses, and e-learning platforms. They have helped bridge the digital divide and democratize access to education.
- **Healthcare:** Mobile phones have had a significant impact on healthcare, particularly in remote areas. They enable telemedicine, remote patient monitoring, and access to health information and services.

Conclusion

Early mobile phones, despite their size and limited capabilities, laid the foundation for the communication devices we rely on today. From the first generation of mobile phones to the advent of smartphones, technological advancements and changing consumer needs have driven the evolution of these devices. Looking back at the early days of mobile telephony provides us with insights into the growth and impact of mobile phones on society.

Rise of Smartphones

The rise of smartphones has revolutionized the way we communicate, access information, and interact with the world around us. In this section, we will explore the evolution of mobile devices, the emergence of smartphones, and their impact on daily life.

Evolution of Mobile Devices

The concept of mobile telephony dates back to the mid-20th century when the first portable phones were introduced. These early mobile phones were large and cumbersome, with limited functionality and high costs. However, they laid the foundation for the development of future mobile devices.

Early Mobile Phones The first commercially available mobile phone was the Motorola DynaTAC 8000X, introduced in 1983. It weighed nearly two pounds and had a price tag of $3,995. While it offered the freedom to make calls on the go, its functionality was limited to basic voice communication.

Over the next decade, mobile phones became smaller, lighter, and more affordable. The introduction of digital cellular networks, such as the Global System for Mobile Communications (GSM), enabled better call quality and increased network capacity. Mobile phones also started to incorporate additional features like text messaging, basic games, and address books.

Rise of Smartphones The term "smartphone" was coined in the late 1990s to describe mobile phones with advanced capabilities beyond voice communication. The emergence of smartphones can be attributed to several key developments:

- **Mobile Operating Systems:** The introduction of mobile operating systems, such as Symbian, BlackBerry OS, and Windows Mobile, enabled the development of third-party applications and enhanced functionality. These operating systems provided a platform for developers to create innovative mobile applications.

- **Advancements in Hardware:** The rapid advancements in hardware technology, including faster processors, larger memory capacities, and better displays, made it possible to perform complex tasks on mobile devices. This facilitated the development of feature-rich smartphones.

- **Mobile Internet Connectivity:** The availability of high-speed mobile internet connectivity, initially through 2G and later 3G and 4G networks, allowed users to access the internet and browse websites on their smartphones. This opened up a wide range of possibilities and services.

Smartphones

Smartphones represent the convergence of communication and computing, offering a wide range of features and capabilities beyond traditional mobile phones.

iOS vs. Android The two dominant mobile operating systems that power smartphones are Apple's iOS and Google's Android. iOS, developed by Apple, is known for its seamless integration with Apple's ecosystem, intuitive user interface, and emphasis on privacy and security. Android, an open-source operating system, is known for its customizability, wide variety of hardware options, and extensive app ecosystem. The fierce competition between iOS and Android has driven innovation and allowed users to choose a platform that best suits their needs.

App Stores and Mobile Applications One of the key aspects that differentiate smartphones from previous mobile devices is the availability of app stores. App stores, such as Apple's App Store and Google Play Store, provide users with a vast selection of applications that can be downloaded and installed on their smartphones. These applications range from productivity tools and social media platforms to entertainment and gaming apps. The app economy has become a thriving industry, with developers earning revenue from app sales and in-app purchases.

Impact of Mobile Computing on Daily Life The widespread adoption of smartphones and mobile computing has had a profound impact on various aspects of daily life. Here are a few examples:

- **Communication:** Smartphones have revolutionized communication by enabling instant messaging, video calls, and social media interaction. People can stay connected with friends and family from anywhere in the world.

- **Information Access:** With smartphones, information is just a few taps away. Users can access news, search for information, and stream videos on the go. This has transformed the way we consume and share information.

- **Mobile Payments and Banking:** Smartphones have become digital wallets, allowing users to make payments, transfer money, and manage their finances. Mobile banking apps have made banking more convenient and accessible.

- **Digital Photography:** The cameras in smartphones have replaced standalone cameras for many users. With the ability to capture high-quality photos and videos, smartphones have democratized photography and made it accessible to everyone.

- **Fitness and Health Tracking:** Smartphones have become personal health assistants, with the ability to track physical activity, monitor heart rate, and provide health-related recommendations. These features have empowered individuals to take control of their well-being.

While smartphones have undoubtedly brought numerous benefits, their pervasive presence has also raised concerns. Issues such as excessive screen time, smartphone addiction, and privacy breaches need to be addressed to ensure a healthy and balanced relationship with mobile technology.

Conclusion

The rise of smartphones has transformed the way we live, work, and interact with the world. These pocket-sized devices have become an essential part of our daily lives, offering communication, entertainment, and productivity at our fingertips.

In this section, we explored the evolution of mobile devices, from the early mobile phones to the emergence of smartphones. We discussed the key developments that led to the rise of smartphones, including the advancements in mobile operating systems, hardware technology, and internet connectivity.

We also delved into the impact of smartphones on daily life, such as their role in communication, access to information, mobile payments, digital photography, and health tracking. However, along with these benefits, the widespread use of smartphones has also brought about new challenges, such as excessive screen time and privacy concerns.

As smartphones continue to evolve and shape our world, it is essential to be mindful of their impact and find a balance between maximizing their potential and maintaining a healthy relationship with technology. The future of smartphones holds exciting possibilities, and we can expect further advancements in areas such as artificial intelligence, augmented reality, and the integration of smartphones with other emerging technologies.

In the next section, we will explore the IBM PC and its role in bringing computing to the masses.

Smartphones

iOS vs. Android

When it comes to mobile operating systems, iOS and Android are the two major players in the market. iOS, developed by Apple, and Android, developed by Google, both offer unique features and experiences for users. In this section, we will compare and contrast the key aspects of iOS and Android, exploring their strengths, weaknesses, and how they have shaped the world of mobile computing.

History and Market Share

iOS was introduced in 2007 with the launch of the first iPhone. It was initially a closed ecosystem, exclusively available on Apple devices such as iPhones, iPads, and iPod Touch. On the other hand, Android was released in 2008 as an open-source operating system, allowing various device manufacturers to use and modify it according to their hardware requirements.

Over the years, both iOS and Android have achieved significant market dominance. As of 2021, Android holds the largest market share globally, accounting for around 72% of the mobile operating system market, while iOS holds around 27%. The broader availability of Android devices across different price ranges and manufacturers has contributed to its larger market share.

User Interface and Design

One of the key differences between iOS and Android is their user interface (UI) and design philosophy. iOS follows a more standardized and cohesive design language known as the Human Interface Guidelines (HIG). It focuses on simplicity, consistency, and ease of use, with a grid-based layout and intuitive gestures.

Android, on the other hand, offers a more customizable and flexible UI. It allows users to personalize their home screens, choose from various widgets, and customize the look and feel of the device. Android also provides different UI skins or overlays by device manufacturers, which can vary in terms of design and functionality.

App Ecosystem

Both iOS and Android have extensive app ecosystems with millions of applications available for download. However, there are differences in how these ecosystems are managed.

The iOS App Store is tightly controlled by Apple, which ensures strict quality control, security, and consistency across apps. All apps go through a review process before being published, which helps maintain a high level of reliability and security. Additionally, iOS apps are generally released first and are often more optimized for the latest features of Apple devices.

Android, on the other hand, follows a more open approach with the Google Play Store. While Google also reviews apps for policy violations and security concerns, the process is less stringent compared to Apple's review process. This allows for a wider range of apps, including those developed by smaller independent developers. Android also allows users to download apps from third-party app stores, further expanding the available options.

Integration with Hardware and Services

iOS is known for its tight integration with Apple's hardware and services ecosystem. Apple controls the entire hardware and software stack, allowing for seamless integration and optimization. This results in a consistent user experience across Apple devices, including features like AirDrop, Handoff, and Continuity, which enable seamless transfer of data and tasks between devices.

Android, being an open-source platform, works on a wide range of hardware devices and is not limited to a single manufacturer. This variety of hardware options allows for more choices in terms of device features, specifications, and pricing. However, due to the fragmentation of hardware and software, not all Android devices have the same level of integration and compatibility with Google's services.

Privacy and Security

Privacy and security are important considerations for mobile users. iOS is often considered to have stronger privacy and security features compared to Android. Apple emphasizes user privacy and employs measures such as end-to-end encryption for messages and data protection through hardware-based encryption. Additionally, Apple's strict app review process ensures that malicious apps are less likely to be available in the App Store.

Android has made significant improvements in privacy and security over the years. Google provides regular security updates to address vulnerabilities and implements privacy-focused features such as app permission controls, Google Play Protect, and the ability to review app permissions. However, due to Android's open nature and the availability of third-party app stores, users may be exposed to a higher risk of malware or privacy issues if they download apps from untrusted sources.

Which is Better: iOS or Android?

The question of whether iOS or Android is better ultimately depends on individual preferences and needs. Here are some factors to consider when choosing between the two:

- **User Experience:** iOS offers a more streamlined and consistent user experience, while Android provides more flexibility and customization options.
- **App Availability:** iOS often receives new app releases first and may have more exclusive apps, whereas Android offers a wider range of apps from various sources.
- **Device Options:** Android provides a wider range of device options across various price ranges and manufacturers, while iOS is limited to Apple devices.
- **Integration and Ecosystem:** iOS provides seamless integration with other Apple devices and services, while Android offers more compatibility with third-party devices and services.
- **Privacy and Security:** iOS is generally considered to have stronger privacy and security features, but Android has improved in these areas and provides more flexibility in controlling app permissions.

Ultimately, the choice between iOS and Android depends on individual preferences, desired features, and the ecosystem one is already invested in (e.g., Apple devices or Google services). Both platforms have their strengths and weaknesses, and the ongoing competition between the two has driven continuous innovation in the world of mobile computing.

Conclusion

In this section, we compared and contrasted iOS and Android, the two major mobile operating systems, highlighting their history, market share, user interface, app ecosystems, integration with hardware and services, and privacy and security aspects. While iOS prioritizes a standardized user experience and strong integration with Apple's ecosystem, Android offers more customization options and a wider range of hardware choices. Choosing between the two ultimately depends on individual preferences, desired features, and the ecosystem in which users are already invested.

App Stores and Mobile Applications

In the ever-evolving world of mobile computing, one of the key factors that has driven its widespread adoption and success is the availability of mobile applications or apps. Mobile applications are software programs designed specifically for use on mobile devices such as smartphones and tablets. They offer a wide range of functionalities, from communication and entertainment to productivity and utility, which have transformed the way we live, work, and interact with the world. The availability and distribution of these apps are made possible through app stores, centralized platforms where users can discover, download, and manage their applications. In this section, we will explore the concept of app stores and delve into the world of mobile applications.

Introduction to App Stores

App stores are digital marketplaces or platforms that enable users to search, discover, and download mobile applications to their devices. These platforms act as intermediaries between app developers and users, providing a convenient and secure way to distribute and access applications. App stores have played a pivotal role in the popularity of mobile applications by offering a centralized location for users to explore and obtain a wide range of apps.

Major App Stores

There are several major app stores in the market today, each with its unique features, guidelines, and user base. Let's take a closer look at some of the prominent app stores:

Apple App Store The Apple App Store, launched in July 2008, was one of the first app stores to revolutionize the mobile application landscape. Available exclusively for Apple devices running iOS, it offers a vast collection of apps across various categories such as games, social networking, productivity, and more. The Apple App Store follows a strict review process to ensure the quality and security of the apps.

Google Play Store The Google Play Store, established in 2008 as Android Market and later rebranded, is the official app store for devices running on the Android operating system. With a massive user base and a wide selection of apps, it caters to a diverse range of interests and needs. The Google Play Store allows developers to choose whether they want to distribute their apps for free or charge a fee. It also includes in-app purchases, where users can buy additional features or content within the app.

Microsoft Store The Microsoft Store, previously known as Windows Store, is the app store for Windows devices, including desktops, laptops, tablets, and smartphones. It offers a range of applications compatible with Windows operating systems, including both traditional Win32 applications and modern Universal Windows Platform (UWP) apps. The Microsoft Store provides a unified experience across different Windows devices and ensures that the apps are secure and reliable.

These are just a few examples of the major app stores available today. Other notable app stores include Amazon Appstore, Samsung Galaxy Store, and Huawei AppGallery, each catering to specific platforms or devices.

App Store Ecosystem

The app store ecosystem comprises app developers, app store operators, and end users, all playing vital roles in shaping the mobile application landscape. Let's take a closer look at each of these stakeholders:

App Developers App developers are the creative minds behind the design, development, and implementation of mobile applications. They write code, design user interfaces, and ensure that the app functions as intended. Developers often face design and development challenges unique to the mobile environment, such as limited screen sizes, resource constraints, and varying hardware capabilities.

App Store Operators App store operators are responsible for managing and maintaining the app store platforms. They review and curate the submitted applications to ensure compliance with guidelines, security standards, and overall quality. App store operators also handle the distribution, monetization, and payment processes, enabling developers to reach a wide user base and generate revenue.

End Users End users are the ultimate beneficiaries of mobile applications. They rely on app stores to discover and download applications that cater to their needs and interests. Users can rate and review apps, helping others make informed decisions about which apps to install. Additionally, app stores offer features like app recommendations, personalized suggestions, and user-generated content to enhance the user experience.

App Development and Guidelines

Developing mobile applications involves understanding a specific set of guidelines provided by app store operators. These guidelines ensure that apps meet certain standards and provide a consistent user experience across different devices and platforms. While the specific guidelines may vary across app stores, here are some common aspects that developers need to consider:

User Interface Design Developers must design intuitive and user-friendly interfaces that comply with the guidelines provided by the app store. This includes considerations for layout, navigation, typography, colors, and other visual elements. Adhering to these guidelines ensures consistency across applications and enhances the overall user experience.

App Permissions Mobile operating systems grant certain permissions to applications to access various device features and resources. For example, access to the camera, microphone, location, and contacts may require specific user permissions. Developers need to explicitly state and justify the need for these permissions in their apps, safeguarding end users' privacy and security.

Security and Data Privacy App store operators enforce stringent security measures to protect users' data and privacy. Developers must implement secure coding practices, handle user data responsibly, and comply with privacy regulations. App stores may reject or remove apps that violate these security and privacy guidelines.

Monetization Strategies

App developers have various monetization options available to generate revenue from their applications. Let's explore some popular strategies used in app stores:

Paid Apps Developers can set a price for their apps, requiring users to purchase them before installation. The revenue generated from purchases allows developers to monetize their efforts directly. To make informed decisions, users often rely on app reviews, ratings, and descriptions provided on the app store.

In-App Purchases In-app purchases allow developers to offer additional content, features, or virtual goods within the app for a fee. This freemium model enables users to download and use the app for free while offering optional purchases for enhanced functionality or premium content. Popular examples include buying virtual currency in games or unlocking advanced features in productivity apps.

Subscription Model The subscription model allows developers to provide ongoing access to their apps' features or content for a recurring fee. This monetization strategy is common in apps that offer news, entertainment, productivity tools, and cloud storage services. Subscriptions provide a steady revenue stream for developers and often include options for monthly or annual billing.

Advertising Advertising is a prevalent monetization strategy in free apps. Developers include ads within their applications, either as banners, interstitials, or rewarded videos. The revenue is generated through impressions, clicks, or interactions with the ads. Advertisements can be displayed within the app's interface or integrated into the app's content.

Challenges and Opportunities

While app stores offer developers a platform for reaching a massive audience and monetizing their applications, there are challenges and opportunities that arise within this ecosystem. Let's explore some of these factors:

Competition and Discoverability With millions of apps available across various app stores, the competition for attention and discoverability is fierce. Getting an app noticed among the vast array of options can be challenging for developers. App store optimization techniques, such as optimizing keywords, screenshots, and descriptions, can help improve an app's visibility and ranking in the search results.

User Reviews and Ratings User reviews and ratings play a significant role in shaping users' perceptions of an app's quality and reliability. Positive reviews and high ratings can boost an app's visibility and attract more users. Conversely, negative reviews and low ratings can impact an app's reputation and discourage potential downloads. Developers must actively manage and respond to user feedback to maintain a positive image.

Device Fragmentation The mobile ecosystem encompasses a wide range of devices with varying screen sizes, operating systems, and hardware capabilities. Ensuring compatibility and optimal performance across this fragmented landscape can be a complex task for developers. They must thoroughly test their apps on different devices and provide sufficient support for compatibility issues.

Emerging Markets and Localization As smartphones and mobile applications continue to penetrate emerging markets, developers have an opportunity to tap into new user bases. However, to succeed globally, localization becomes crucial. Adapting the app's language, content, and cultural elements to specific regions can significantly improve user engagement and adoption.

Conclusion

App stores and mobile applications have transformed the way we use technology and interact with the digital world. These platforms have democratized software distribution, allowing developers to reach a global audience and users to access a vast array of applications. The success of mobile computing owes much to the convenience, versatility, and innovation brought about by app stores and the applications within them. As the mobile landscape continues to evolve, app stores will play a pivotal role in shaping the future of mobile applications and their impact on society.

Impact of Mobile Computing on Daily Life

The advent of mobile computing has revolutionized the way we live, work, and communicate in the modern world. Mobile devices, such as smartphones and tablets, have become an integral part of our daily lives, offering unprecedented convenience and accessibility. In this section, we will explore the profound impact of mobile computing on various aspects of our daily life.

Communication and Connectivity

Mobile computing has transformed the way we communicate with each other. With the availability of smartphones, we can now stay connected to our friends, family, and colleagues from anywhere in the world. Mobile apps and instant messaging platforms allow us to send text messages, make voice and video calls, and share multimedia content effortlessly.

Social networking sites, such as Facebook, Twitter, and Instagram, have gained immense popularity, offering a platform for people to connect and share their thoughts, experiences, and emotions in real-time. Mobile computing has made it easier to maintain social relationships, even across long distances, by bridging the gap of time and space.

Moreover, mobile computing has greatly enhanced the efficiency and effectiveness of business communication. Emails, calendar apps, and project management tools enable professionals to stay organized, collaborate remotely, and respond promptly to work-related matters. With cloud storage and document sharing services, teams can access and edit files seamlessly, regardless of their physical location.

Information and Entertainment

Mobile computing has transformed the way we access information and consume media. With the internet at our fingertips, we can instantly retrieve information on a wide range of topics, from news and weather updates to research papers and educational resources. Mobile apps and websites provide access to e-books, online courses, and tutorials, allowing us to acquire knowledge anytime, anywhere.

Streaming services, such as Netflix, Spotify, and YouTube, have revolutionized the entertainment industry. Mobile devices enable us to enjoy music, movies, TV shows, and videos on the go, eliminating the need for traditional media formats. With personalized recommendations and offline capabilities, mobile apps have made entertainment more accessible, personalized, and immersive.

The rise of mobile gaming has introduced a new form of entertainment, offering a wide range of interactive and engaging experiences. Mobile games have become increasingly sophisticated, with advanced graphics, multiplayer capabilities, and augmented reality features. They provide a form of relaxation, socialization, and escapism in our daily lives.

Productivity and Lifestyle

Mobile computing has greatly enhanced our productivity and efficiency, enabling us to perform a multitude of tasks without being tied to a desk. Mobile apps, such as note-taking tools, task managers, and calendars, help us stay organized, manage our time effectively, and track our progress on various projects and goals.

E-commerce has experienced significant growth with the rise of mobile computing. Online shopping apps allow us to browse and purchase products from the comfort of our homes or on the go. Mobile payment systems and digital wallets facilitate secure and convenient transactions, reducing the need for physical cash and cards.

Health and fitness apps have gained popularity, helping us monitor our physical activity, track our diet, and manage our overall well-being. Mobile devices equipped with sensors and wearable fitness trackers provide real-time feedback and motivation, encouraging us to lead healthier lifestyles.

Mobile computing has also revolutionized the travel and transportation industry. Mobile apps, such as ride-sharing services and navigation tools, provide real-time information on routes, traffic conditions, and public transportation schedules. They have made commuting more convenient, efficient, and environmentally friendly.

Challenges and Concerns

While the impact of mobile computing on daily life has been overwhelmingly positive, it also brings forth certain challenges and concerns. One major concern is the addiction and overreliance on mobile devices, leading to decreased social interaction, sleep disturbances, and reduced productivity. It is important to find a balance and practice healthy digital habits to avoid the detrimental effects of excessive mobile device usage.

Privacy and security are also significant concerns in the mobile computing era. With the proliferation of personal data on mobile devices and the internet, there is an increased risk of data breaches, identity theft, and unauthorized access to sensitive information. It is crucial to be vigilant, use strong passwords, and employ security measures, such as encryption and two-factor authentication, to protect our personal data.

Furthermore, the digital divide remains a challenge, as not everyone has equal access to mobile devices and internet connectivity. This can create disparities in education, employment opportunities, and access to essential services. Efforts should be made to bridge this gap and ensure digital inclusion for all members of society.

Conclusion

Mobile computing has had a profound impact on our daily lives, revolutionizing communication, access to information, entertainment, productivity, and lifestyle. It has transformed the way we interact with others, consume media, conduct business, and live our lives. While enjoying the benefits of mobile computing, it is essential to be mindful of its challenges and concerns, such as addiction, privacy, and the digital divide. As mobile technology continues to evolve, it holds tremendous potential to shape the future and further enhance our daily experiences.

Tablets and Wearable Devices

iPad and the Tablet Revolution

The introduction of the iPad in 2010 marked a significant milestone in the history of computing and sparked a new era of mobile computing. The iPad, a tablet device developed by Apple Inc., revolutionized the way people interact with technology and paved the way for a new category of devices that bridge the gap between smartphones and traditional computers.

Background

Tablet computers have a long history that dates back to the early 1990s, with Microsoft's release of the Windows for Pen Computing operating system. However, these early attempts at tablet computing were met with limited success due to technological limitations and the lack of a compelling user experience. It was not until the release of the iPad that tablets gained mainstream popularity and became a viable computing option for consumers.

Key Features of the iPad

The iPad introduced several key features that contributed to its success and the subsequent tablet revolution:

- **Multi-touch interface:** The iPad featured a large, high-resolution touchscreen display that allowed users to interact with the device using gestures, such as tapping, swiping, and pinching. This intuitive and natural user interface made the iPad easy to use and accessible to a wide range of users.
- **Portability:** The iPad was lightweight and portable, making it convenient for users to carry and use the device on the go. Its compact form factor, combined with its long battery life, made it a popular choice for travelers, students, and professionals.
- **App ecosystem:** The iPad introduced the concept of mobile apps, which could be downloaded from the App Store and installed on the device. This vast ecosystem of applications provided users with a wide range of functionality, including productivity tools, entertainment content, and creative applications.
- **Media consumption:** The iPad excelled as a media consumption device, allowing users to browse the internet, watch videos, listen to music, and read books and magazines. Its large display and high-quality graphics made it a popular choice for multimedia content consumption.

Impact on Computing

The iPad and the tablet revolution it ignited had a profound impact on various aspects of computing:

1. **Mobile Computing:** The iPad popularized the concept of mobile computing, providing users with a portable and convenient device for accessing information, staying connected, and performing essential tasks. It paved the way for the emergence of a wide range of tablets from various manufacturers, offering consumers more choice and driving innovation in the mobile computing space.

2. **Changing Computing Habits:** The iPad challenged traditional computing habits by offering a new form factor and user experience. Its touch-based interface and app-centric approach influenced the design and development of both mobile and desktop operating systems, leading to the adoption of touchscreens and app stores in other computing devices.

3. **Digital Transformation:** The iPad played a significant role in the digital transformation of industries such as education, healthcare, and retail. It provided new opportunities for immersive digital learning, telemedicine, and mobile point-of-sale systems, revolutionizing the way these industries operate and interact with their customers.

4. **Ecosystem Integration:** The success of the iPad and its integration with Apple's ecosystem of devices and services, such as iCloud and iTunes, further solidified Apple's presence in the digital market. It encouraged users to adopt other Apple products, such as iPhones and Macs, creating a seamless and interconnected user experience across multiple devices.

Challenges and Limitations

Despite its enormous success, the iPad and the tablet market faced several challenges and limitations:

- **Productivity vs. Consumption:** While the iPad excelled as a media consumption device, its productivity capabilities were initially limited. The lack of a physical keyboard, limited multitasking capabilities, and the absence of specialized software hindered its adoption as a primary computing device for tasks such as content creation, programming, and data analysis.

- **Competition and Market Saturation:** As the tablet market expanded, numerous competitors released their own offerings, leading to increased competition and market saturation. Android tablets, Windows tablets, and other competing platforms gained traction, challenging the iPad's dominance and forcing Apple to continually innovate to maintain its market share.

- **Price Point and Affordability:** The initial price of the iPad and subsequent models positioned it as a premium device, limiting its accessibility for price-conscious consumers, particularly in emerging markets. Although the entry-level models became more affordable over time, the cost of accessories and software could still be a barrier for some users.

Future Directions

The iPad and the tablet market continue to evolve, with several trends and developments shaping their future:

1. **Hybrid Devices:** The line between tablets and traditional laptops has become increasingly blurred, with the emergence of hybrid devices that offer a combination of touchscreens, detachable keyboards, and convertible form factors. These devices aim to provide the versatility and

portability of tablets while offering the productivity and functionality of laptops.

2. **Improved Productivity:** Tablet manufacturers are focusing on enhancing the productivity capabilities of their devices by improving multitasking, introducing stylus support for precise input, and developing specialized software for tasks such as content creation and video editing. This push for increased productivity aims to position tablets as viable alternatives to traditional laptops in a wider range of professional use cases.

3. **Advancements in Display Technology:** The development of high-resolution displays, such as OLED and microLED, and advancements in touch and pen input technologies are expected to enhance the user experience and expand the capabilities of tablets. These advancements may include features like improved color accuracy, increased refresh rates, and support for advanced stylus functionalities.

4. **Integration with 5G and Internet of Things (IoT):** The integration of tablets with 5G networks and IoT devices will enable new use cases and opportunities for connectivity. Tablets can serve as control centers for smart homes, IoT hubs for managing connected devices, and portable productivity tools with ultra-fast internet connectivity.

Conclusion

The iPad and the tablet revolution it initiated have had a lasting impact on the computing landscape. Its introduction brought about a new era of mobile computing, changed computing habits, and transformed various industries. While the tablet market has faced challenges and limitations, ongoing advancements and innovations continue to drive the evolution of tablets, making them more versatile, powerful, and essential tools for both personal and professional use.

The iPad and the tablet revolution remind us that technology is continually evolving, and new form factors and user experiences can shape the future of computing. As we embrace the possibilities offered by tablets and other emerging technologies, it is vital to consider their ethical and social implications and work towards creating a more inclusive, secure, and sustainable digital future.

Smartwatches and Fitness Trackers

With the rapid advancement of technology, smartwatches and fitness trackers have become increasingly popular among users of all ages. These wearable devices have revolutionized the way we track and monitor our health and fitness goals. In this section, we will explore the features and capabilities of smartwatches and fitness trackers, as well as their impact on daily life and overall well-being.

Functionality and Features

Smartwatches and fitness trackers are designed to be worn on the wrist and offer a variety of features to help users stay connected, organized, and motivated to maintain a healthy lifestyle. Some common features include:

- **Fitness Tracking:** Smartwatches and fitness trackers are equipped with sensors that can track various physical activities, such as steps taken, distance traveled, calories burned, and even heart rate. These devices provide valuable insights into our daily activity levels and encourage us to make healthier choices.

- **Heart Rate Monitoring:** By continuously monitoring our heart rate, smartwatches and fitness trackers can provide real-time feedback on our cardiovascular health. This feature is particularly useful during workouts, allowing us to optimize our exercise intensity and ensure that we are working within our target heart rate zones.
- **Sleep Tracking:** Many smartwatches and fitness trackers also include sleep tracking capabilities. By monitoring our sleep patterns, these devices can provide valuable information about the quality and duration of our sleep, helping us make necessary adjustments to improve our overall sleep hygiene.
- **Notifications and Connectivity:** Smartwatches can be synced with our smartphones, allowing us to receive notifications for calls, messages, and social media alerts directly on our wrists. This feature ensures that we remain connected and informed, even when our phones are not easily accessible.
- **GPS and Navigation:** Some advanced smartwatches include built-in GPS functionality, which allows us to track our outdoor activities accurately. This feature is particularly useful for runners and cyclists who want to monitor their routes, distance, and pace in real-time.

Impact on Health and Fitness

Smartwatches and fitness trackers have had a significant impact on promoting a healthy lifestyle and improving overall fitness levels. Here are some ways these devices have influenced our health and well-being:

- **Encouragement and Motivation:** The ability to track our daily activities, set fitness goals, and receive feedback in real-time can be highly motivating. Smartwatches and fitness trackers provide a sense of achievement and encourage us to stay active and make healthier choices.

- **Accountability and Progress Tracking:** With the help of these devices, we can easily monitor our progress and track our workouts. This accountability factor helps us stay on track and make adjustments to our routines to achieve our fitness goals more effectively.

- **Sleep and Stress Management:** The sleep tracking feature in smartwatches and fitness trackers has raised awareness about the importance of good sleep hygiene. By providing insights into our sleep patterns, these devices enable us to make lifestyle changes that can positively impact our sleep quality and overall well-being. Some devices also offer stress management features, such as guided breathing exercises, to help us relax and manage stress more effectively.

- **Prevention and Early Detection:** Continuous heart rate monitoring can serve as an early indicator of potential health issues. If abnormalities or irregularities are detected, smartwatches and fitness trackers can alert us to seek medical attention promptly, potentially preventing more serious health conditions.

- **Community and Social Support:** Many smartwatches and fitness trackers offer social features that allow users to connect, compete, and engage with others who have similar fitness goals. This sense of community and support can be highly motivating and help individuals stay committed to their fitness routines.

Limitations and Considerations

While smartwatches and fitness trackers offer numerous benefits, it is important to be aware of their limitations and consider certain factors before incorporating them into our daily lives:

- **Accuracy and Reliability:** While these devices have become increasingly accurate, they may still have limitations in terms of their measurements. Factors such as placement, motion, and user characteristics can affect the accuracy of the data collected. It is crucial to interpret the information provided by these devices as estimates rather than precise measurements.

- **Battery Life:** Smartwatches and fitness trackers require regular charging. Battery life varies depending on the device and usage patterns, so it is essential to consider battery life when selecting a device to ensure it meets our needs and preferences.

- **Data Privacy and Security:** Wearable devices, like smartwatches and fitness trackers, collect and store personal data about our health and fitness. It is important to choose devices from reputable manufacturers and be mindful of data privacy and security measures to protect our personal information.

- **Physical Comfort and Design:** Since these devices are meant to be worn throughout the day, it is crucial to consider factors such as comfort, fit, and design. Different individuals may have different preferences, so it is important to choose a device that feels comfortable and suits our style and needs.

Example

To illustrate the capabilities of smartwatches and fitness trackers, let's consider an example. Sarah recently purchased a fitness tracker to help her achieve her health and fitness goals. After wearing the device for a week, she noticed that it accurately tracked her steps throughout the day, motivating her to increase her daily activity levels. Additionally, the sleep tracking feature provided insights into her sleep quality and duration, encouraging her to establish a consistent sleep routine. With the integration of a heart rate monitor, Sarah was able to monitor her cardiovascular health during workouts, allowing her to optimize her exercise intensity and stay within her target heart rate zone.

Resources

If you are interested in learning more about smartwatches and fitness trackers, here are some additional resources:

- *Smartwatches for Dummies* by NextYoo, et al.
- *Fitness Trackers: A Comprehensive Guide* by FitLife Magazine
- Website: How to Choose the Right Smartwatch for Your Needs (www.smartwatchguide.com)
- Website: The Best Fitness Trackers of [current year] (www.fitnesstracker.io)

Conclusion

Smartwatches and fitness trackers have transformed the way we approach health and fitness. These devices provide valuable insights into our daily activities, sleep patterns, heart health, and more. By leveraging the features of smartwatches and fitness trackers, we can stay motivated, track our progress, and make informed decisions to improve our overall well-being. As technology continues to evolve, we can expect even more advanced features and capabilities from these wearable devices in the future, further enhancing our health and fitness journeys. So, get ready to embrace the power of smartwatches and fitness trackers in your quest for a healthier lifestyle!

Artificial Intelligence

Early AI Concepts

Dartmouth Workshop and the Birth of AI

The Dartmouth Workshop, held in the summer of 1956, is widely regarded as the birthplace of artificial intelligence (AI). This historic event brought together researchers from various disciplines, including computer science, mathematics, psychology, and engineering. The workshop aimed to explore the possibilities of creating an "electronic brain" that could replicate human intelligence.

Motivation and Goals

The Dartmouth Workshop was a direct response to the belief that computers could be more than mere number-crunching machines. Researchers were intrigued by the idea of creating machines that could exhibit human-like intelligence and solve complex problems. The workshop aimed to lay the foundations for a new field of study that focused on creating intelligent machines.

The workshop's primary goals were to develop programs capable of performing tasks such as language translation, pattern recognition, and problem-solving. These tasks were chosen because they represented some of the core cognitive abilities associated with human intelligence. The researchers envisioned that by understanding and implementing these abilities in machines, they could pave the way for the development of truly intelligent systems.

Turing Test

One of the key discussions during the Dartmouth Workshop revolved around the concept of a machine's ability to exhibit intelligent behavior. Alan Turing, a British mathematician and computer scientist, proposed a test that would later become known as the Turing Test. The test aimed to determine whether a machine could convincingly imitate human intelligence.

According to the Turing Test, if a machine's responses were indistinguishable from those of a human, then it could be considered as intelligent as a human. This concept sparked a great deal of debate and became a central focus of the workshop's discussions. While there was no definitive conclusion on the viability of the Turing Test, it paved the way for future research in AI and remains a crucial aspect of the field to this day.

Early AI Systems

Although the Dartmouth Workshop did not produce any groundbreaking AI systems, it set the stage for the development of early AI programs. One of the notable projects to emerge from the workshop was the Logic Theorist, created by Allen Newell and Herbert A. Simon. The Logic Theorist used a set of predefined rules to prove mathematical theorems, demonstrating the potential for machines to perform human-like reasoning.

Another significant project was the General Problem Solver (GPS), developed by Newell, Simon, and J.C. Shaw. GPS aimed to solve a wide range of complex problems by breaking them down into smaller sub-problems and iteratively applying problem-solving techniques. Although GPS had limited success, it established the foundation for future work in problem-solving and planning.

Limitations and Challenges

During the Dartmouth Workshop, researchers recognized several challenges and limitations associated with AI. One primary challenge was the lack of computational power at the time. Computers were relatively slow and had limited memory capacity, making it difficult to implement complex AI algorithms.

Another challenge was the limited availability of data. AI systems heavily rely on data to learn and make informed decisions. In the 1950s, there was a lack of large-scale datasets that could be used to train and test AI models.

Furthermore, researchers struggled with the fundamental question of what constitutes intelligence. Defining intelligent behavior and implementing it in machines proved to be a complex and multifaceted task. The workshop highlighted the need for a unified theoretical framework that could guide the development of AI systems.

Impact and Legacy

The Dartmouth Workshop served as a catalyst for the emergence of the field of AI. It brought together researchers who would go on to become influential figures in AI research, including John McCarthy, Marvin Minsky, Nathaniel Rochester, and Claude Shannon. These researchers continued to work on AI and contributed to its growth and development.

The workshop also inspired subsequent conferences and research initiatives focused on AI. It paved the way for the establishment of AI as a distinct scientific discipline, leading to the formation of dedicated AI research centers and departments at universities worldwide.

Today, AI has become an integral part of our daily lives, with applications ranging from voice assistants and self-driving cars to medical diagnosis and financial forecasting. The foundational work and discussions at the Dartmouth Workshop laid the groundwork for the advancements in AI that we see today.

Resources and Further Reading

For those interested in delving deeper into the topic, the following resources provide additional information on the Dartmouth Workshop and the birth of AI:

- McCarthy, J., Minsky, M. L., Rochester, N., & Shannon, C. E. (1955). A Proposal for the Dartmouth Summer Research Project on Artificial Intelligence. Retrieved from `https://aaai.org/ojs/index.php/aimagazine/article/view/1904`
- McCorduck, P. (2004). Machines Who Think: A Personal Inquiry into the History and Prospects of Artificial Intelligence. A K Peters/CRC Press.
- Dartmouth College. (2021). The Dartmouth Workshop. Retrieved from `https://ai.dartmouth.edu/events/dartmouth-ai-conf`

By exploring these resources, readers can gain a comprehensive understanding of the Dartmouth Workshop and its significant role in the birth of AI.

Turing Test: Assessing Machine Intelligence

The Turing Test, proposed by the brilliant mathematician and computer scientist Alan Turing in 1950, is one of the most famous tests used to evaluate the intelligence of a machine. It serves as a benchmark for assessing the ability of a computer program to exhibit human-like behavior.

Background

To understand the significance of the Turing Test, it is essential to grasp Turing's concept of machine intelligence. Turing believed that intelligence was not exclusive to humans but could be replicated in machines. He proposed that if a machine could generate responses indistinguishable from those of a human, it could be considered intelligent.

The underlying idea behind the Turing Test is that a machine should be able to mimic human conversations to the extent that the human evaluator cannot distinguish it from another human. In this test, a human evaluator engages in a conversation with both a machine and another human via a computer interface. If the evaluator cannot reliably distinguish between the machine and the human, then the machine is said to have passed the test.

The Test Process

The Turing Test consists of three participants: the machine being tested (referred to as the "test subject"), a human evaluator, and a human control. The evaluator's task is to converse with both the test subject and the control subject (another human) through a chat interface without any visual or physical cues. The evaluator's goal is to determine which participant is human and which is the machine.

The test is typically conducted using a text-based interface to focus solely on language understanding and generation abilities. To ensure unbiased judgment, the evaluator is kept unaware of the identity of the participants.

The Challenges

Developing a machine capable of passing the Turing Test is a formidable challenge due to several reasons:

- Natural Language Understanding: The machine must possess advanced natural language processing capabilities to understand the nuances and subtleties of human language.
- Contextual Understanding: The ability to understand and appropriately respond to context is crucial for passing the Turing Test. It requires the machine to comprehend and retain information from previous parts of the conversation.
- Creativity and Humor: Demonstrating creativity and the ability to appreciate and generate humor is a significant marker of human-like intelligence. The machine must be able to go beyond simple factual responses and provide creative and witty responses.
- General Knowledge: A well-rounded general knowledge base is essential for the machine to engage in diverse topics of conversation effectively.
- Emotional Intelligence: Emulating emotions in conversation is an essential aspect of human-like intelligence. The machine must be able to demonstrate empathy, understanding, and appropriate emotional responses.

Limitations and Criticisms

The Turing Test, despite its significance, has faced its share of criticisms. Some argue that it is more of a test of human gullibility rather than machine intelligence. A machine could potentially deceive the evaluator by cleverly masking its lack of true understanding through superficial responses.

Furthermore, passing the Turing Test does not necessarily equate to genuine intelligence. The ability to mimic human behavior does not guarantee the machine's comprehension or conscious thought.

Contemporary Relevance

The Turing Test remains relevant today as the field of artificial intelligence (AI) continues to advance. Researchers actively explore and refine conversational agents to enhance their linguistic and reasoning capabilities. The test acts as a valuable benchmark for evaluating the progress of AI systems, pushing the boundaries of their capabilities.

Moreover, the Turing Test has sparked debates on the nature of intelligence and what it means to be human. It challenges us to reflect on the fundamental characteristics that define human intelligence and explore the ethical implications of creating machines that exhibit human-like behavior.

Examples and Applications

The Turing Test has been the inspiration for various competitions and challenges aimed at assessing AI capabilities. One notable example is the Loebner Prize, an annual competition where chatbots compete to convince human judges that they are indistinguishable from humans.

The principles of the Turing Test also extend beyond conversational AI. It has influenced the development of AI systems for applications such as customer service chatbots, virtual assistants, recommendation systems, and more. These systems strive to provide natural, human-like interactions to enhance user experience.

Further Reading

To delve deeper into the topic of the Turing Test and its implications, the following resources are recommended:

- "Alan Turing: The Enigma" by Andrew Hodges. This biography provides insights into Alan Turing's life and his influential contributions to computer science and AI, including the Turing Test.
- "The Most Human Human: What Talking with Computers Teaches Us About What It Means to Be Alive" by Brian Christian. This book explores the intricacies of human communication and the Turing Test through the author's participation in the Loebner Prize competition.
- "Superintelligence: Paths, Dangers, Strategies" by Nick Bostrom. This thought-provoking book delves into the future of AI and its potential implications for society, raising questions about the very nature of intelligence.

Exercises

To test your understanding of the Turing Test, consider the following exercises:

1. Imagine you are an evaluator in a Turing Test. Design a set of questions and conversations that would effectively challenge both the human and machine participants.
2. Research and discuss the criticisms and debates surrounding the Turing Test. Are there alternative assessments that could provide a more comprehensive evaluation of machine intelligence?

3. Explore the current state of conversational AI systems. Identify and evaluate one example of a chatbot or virtual assistant that aims to pass the Turing Test. Assess its strengths and limitations in mimicking human-like conversation.

Remember, the Turing Test not only assesses the capabilities of AI but also prompts us to ponder the essence of human intelligence and the ethical implications of replicating it in machines.

Good luck!

Machine Learning and Neural Networks

Early Neural Network Research

Neural networks, inspired by the working of the human brain, have become an essential part of modern artificial intelligence (AI). In this section, we explore the early research carried out in the field of neural networks, laying the foundation for the development of this powerful technique.

McCulloch-Pitts Neuron Model

The earliest theoretical model of a neuron was proposed by Warren McCulloch and Walter Pitts in 1943. Their model, known as the McCulloch-Pitts (M-P) neuron, provided a simplified representation of the biological neuron and introduced the concept of computational units that would later form the basis of neural networks.

The M-P neuron takes binary inputs and produces a binary output based on a set of weighted connections and a threshold. The inputs are summed with their corresponding weights, and if the sum exceeds the threshold, the neuron fires, producing an output of 1; otherwise, it remains inactive, with an output of 0. The M-P neuron can be represented mathematically as:

$$y = \begin{cases} 1, & \text{if } \sum_{i=1}^{n} w_i x_i \geq \theta \\ 0, & \text{otherwise} \end{cases}$$

where x_i represents the input, w_i represents the corresponding weight, and θ represents the threshold.

Perceptron Learning Algorithm

In 1957, Frank Rosenblatt introduced the perceptron learning algorithm, which gave rise to the development of the perceptron, a type of neural network. The perceptron learning algorithm addresses the problem of finding the optimal weights for a set of inputs to obtain the desired output.

The algorithm adjusts the weights based on the error between the predicted output and the desired output. By iteratively updating the weights, the perceptron learns to classify input patterns correctly. The weight update rule can be mathematically represented as:

$$w_{i+1} = w_i + \alpha \cdot (d - y) \cdot x_i$$

where w_i and w_{i+1} represent the weights at iteration i and $i + 1$ respectively, x_i represents the input, d represents the desired output, y represents the predicted output, and α represents the learning rate.

Despite its limited capabilities, the perceptron learning algorithm laid the groundwork for further advancements in neural network research.

Limitations and Controversies

Early neural network research faced limitations and controversies, hindering its progress. One prominent limitation was the perceptron's inability to classify patterns that were not linearly separable. For example, a perceptron cannot solve the XOR problem, where inputs with different values result in the same output. This limitation led to concerns about the practical applications of neural networks.

Another controversy arose from the perception among some researchers that perceptron-based neural networks were biologically unrealistic, as they oversimplified the complexities of the brain's neural architecture. These concerns resulted in a decline in neural network research and the dominance of alternative AI approaches, such as rule-based systems and expert systems.

Rebirth of Neural Networks

Despite the initial setbacks, neural network research experienced a rejuvenation in the 1980s due to the development of new algorithms and the availability of more computational resources.

One breakthrough was the introduction of backpropagation, an algorithm for training multi-layer feedforward neural networks. Paul Werbos first proposed the concept of backpropagation in 1974, but it gained wider recognition in the late 1980s when researchers demonstrated its effectiveness in training neural networks.

Backpropagation calculates the gradient of the error function with respect to the weights of the neural network, allowing for the adjustment of weights through gradient descent. This algorithm enabled neural networks to successfully classify non-linearly separable patterns, expanding their capabilities and enhancing their practical applications.

Emerging Applications

The progress made in neural network research opened up a wide range of applications. Neural networks have been applied in various domains, including image and speech recognition, natural language processing, pattern recognition, forecasting, and decision-making systems.

One notable application is the use of neural networks in autonomous vehicles. Neural networks enable self-driving cars to accurately recognize and classify objects, make decisions based on real-time traffic data, and navigate complex road conditions.

Furthermore, neural networks have revolutionized healthcare by assisting in medical diagnoses, predicting patient outcomes, and analyzing large volumes of medical data. They have also been instrumental in financial forecasting, fraud detection, and recommendation systems in e-commerce platforms.

Conclusion

Early research in neural networks, starting with the McCulloch-Pitts neuron model and the perceptron learning algorithm, laid the foundation for the development of this powerful AI technique. Despite initial limitations and controversies, advancements such as backpropagation propelled neural networks to the forefront of AI research. Today, neural networks find diverse applications, transforming industries and reshaping the technological landscape.

Summary

In this section, we explored the early research in the field of neural networks. We discussed the McCulloch-Pitts neuron model, which provided a theoretical framework for computational units in neural networks. We also examined the perceptron learning algorithm, which introduced a method for adjusting weights to achieve the desired output. Despite limitations and controversies, the field experienced a rebirth with the introduction of backpropagation, enabling the training of multi-layer neural networks. We concluded by highlighting the wide range of emerging applications of neural networks in various domains.

Backpropagation Algorithm

The Backpropagation algorithm is a critical component of training neural networks, enabling them to learn from data and improve their performance over time. It is a supervised learning algorithm that adjusts the weights and biases of a neural network based on the error between the predicted output and the correct output.

The Need for Backpropagation

Before diving into the details of the Backpropagation algorithm, let's first understand the motivation behind it. Neural networks are composed of multiple layers of interconnected nodes called neurons, and these neurons work together to process input data and generate output predictions. During the training process, the neural network is presented with a set of input-output pairs, and it attempts to learn the mapping between the inputs and the corresponding outputs.

The key challenge in training neural networks is determining how to update the weights and biases of the neurons to minimize the error between the predicted output and the desired output. This is where the Backpropagation algorithm comes into play.

Overview of the Backpropagation Algorithm

The Backpropagation algorithm is based on the chain rule of calculus, which allows us to compute the partial derivatives of the error with respect to the weights and biases in each layer of the neural network. By considering the error contribution of each neuron in the network, we can determine how much each weight and bias needs to be adjusted to reduce the overall error.

The algorithm works in two main steps: forward propagation and backward propagation. During forward propagation, the input is fed through the network, and the output is computed. During backward propagation, the error is propagated back through the network, and the weights and biases are updated based on the gradients of the error with respect to these parameters.

Forward Propagation

In the forward propagation step, each neuron receives input from the previous layer and computes its output using an activation function. The output of each neuron is then passed as input to the next layer until the final output is generated.

Mathematically, we can represent the forward propagation step as follows:

$$\text{Input} : \mathbf{X} = [x_1, x_2, \ldots, x_n] \tag{1}$$

$$\text{Hidden layer output} : \mathbf{H} = \sigma(\mathbf{W}_1 \cdot \mathbf{X} + \mathbf{b}_1) \tag{2}$$

$$\text{Output} : \mathbf{Y} = \sigma(\mathbf{W}_2 \cdot \mathbf{H} + \mathbf{b}_2) \tag{3}$$

where σ represents the activation function, $\mathbf{W}_1$ and $\mathbf{W}_2$ are the weight matrices of the first and second layers respectively, $\mathbf{b}_1$ and $\mathbf{b}_2$ are the bias vectors, and $\mathbf{H}$ and $\mathbf{Y}$ are the outputs of the hidden and output layers.

Backward Propagation

In the backward propagation step, the error is computed by comparing the predicted output with the desired output. This error is then propagated back through the network, layer by layer, to compute the gradients of the error with respect to the weights and biases.

To update the weights and biases, we use an optimization algorithm such as gradient descent. The gradients calculated during backward propagation indicate the direction in which the weights and biases should be adjusted to minimize the error.

Mathematically, the update equations for the weights and biases in the backward propagation step are as follows:

$$\Delta \mathbf{W}_2 = -\eta \frac{\partial E}{\partial \mathbf{W}_2} \tag{4}$$

$$\Delta \mathbf{b}_2 = -\eta \frac{\partial E}{\partial \mathbf{b}_2} \tag{5}$$

$$\Delta \mathbf{W}_1 = -\eta \frac{\partial E}{\partial \mathbf{W}_1} \tag{6}$$

$$\Delta \mathbf{b}_1 = -\eta \frac{\partial E}{\partial \mathbf{b}_1} \tag{7}$$

where η represents the learning rate, and $\frac{\partial E}{\partial \mathbf{W}_2}$, $\frac{\partial E}{\partial \mathbf{b}_2}$, $\frac{\partial E}{\partial \mathbf{W}_1}$, and $\frac{\partial E}{\partial \mathbf{b}_1}$ are the gradients of the error with respect to the weights and biases.

Training Process

The training process involves iteratively applying forward and backward propagation to update the weights and biases of the neural network. This process continues until the error is minimized, and the network achieves satisfactory performance on the training data.

Here is a step-by-step summary of the training process using the Backpropagation algorithm:

1. Initialize the weights and biases of the neural network randomly. 2. Feed the input data through the network using forward propagation, and compute the output. 3. Compare the predicted output with the desired output and calculate the error. 4. Use backward propagation to compute the gradients of the error with respect to the weights and biases. 5. Update the weights and biases using an optimization algorithm (e.g., gradient descent). 6. Repeat steps 2-5 for all training examples in the dataset. 7. Repeat steps 2-6 for multiple epochs until the error is minimized.

Challenges and Tricks

Training neural networks using the Backpropagation algorithm can be challenging due to several reasons, such as the vanishing gradient problem or overfitting. However, researchers have developed several techniques to address these challenges and improve the performance of the algorithm.

One such technique is the use of activation functions that prevent the vanishing gradient problem, such as the Rectified Linear Unit (ReLU) function. Additionally, regularization techniques like dropout and weight decay can help prevent overfitting by reducing the complexity of the neural network.

Furthermore, the choice of the learning rate is crucial for successful training. A learning rate that is too high can cause the training process to diverge, while a learning rate that is too low can result in slow convergence. Adaptive learning rate algorithms, such as the Adam optimizer, can automatically adjust the learning rate during training and improve convergence.

Conclusion

The Backpropagation algorithm is a fundamental technique for training neural networks. It enables the network to learn from data and improve its performance over time. By iteratively adjusting the weights and biases of the network based on the error, the algorithm allows the network to approximate complex functions and make accurate predictions.

Although the Backpropagation algorithm has its challenges, researchers and practitioners continue to develop new techniques and improvements to make it more efficient and effective. It remains a cornerstone in the field of artificial intelligence and has played a significant role in the success of neural networks in various applications.

Evolution of Machine Learning Paradigms

Machine learning is a rapidly evolving field that has seen significant advancements in recent years. In this section, we will explore the evolution of machine learning paradigms, tracing the development of various approaches and techniques that have shaped the field. We will discuss the historical context, key milestones, and current trends in machine learning.

Traditional Approaches

The early days of machine learning were characterized by traditional approaches that relied on statistical methods and heuristics. These approaches aimed to build models that could generalize from observed data and make predictions or decisions.

Statistical Learning Theory: One of the foundational concepts in machine learning is statistical learning theory. Developed in the 1960s, statistical learning theory focused on the analysis of statistical models and the formulation of learning algorithms. This theory laid the groundwork for many subsequent developments in machine learning.

Supervised Learning: Supervised learning, also known as predictive modeling, is a paradigm where the model is trained on labeled examples to learn a mapping between input data and output labels. The goal is to generalize the learned mapping to unseen data. Examples of supervised learning algorithms include decision trees, support vector machines, and neural networks.

Unsupervised Learning: Unsupervised learning, on the other hand, involves training models on unlabeled data to discover hidden patterns or representations in the data. Clustering, dimensionality reduction, and generative models are common examples of unsupervised learning techniques.

Reinforcement Learning: Reinforcement learning is a paradigm that involves an agent learning to make decisions in an environment to maximize some notion of cumulative reward. The agent learns through trial and error, receiving feedback in the form of rewards or penalties. Reinforcement learning has been successfully applied to problems such as game playing, robotics, and optimization.

Deep Learning Revolution

In recent years, deep learning, a subfield of machine learning, has emerged as a dominant paradigm, revolutionizing many areas of AI research. Deep learning models, based on artificial neural networks with multiple layers, have achieved remarkable performance on numerous tasks, including image recognition, speech synthesis, and natural language processing.

Neural Networks: Neural networks are computational models inspired by biological neural networks. They consist of interconnected nodes, or "neurons," that process and transmit information. The nodes are organized into layers, with each layer transforming the input in a non-linear manner. Deep neural networks, with many layers, have the ability to learn increasingly complex representations of the input data.

Convolutional Neural Networks: Convolutional neural networks (CNNs) are a specialized type of neural network designed for processing grid-like data such as images. They utilize convolutional layers, which apply filters to locally connected regions of the input, enabling the network to automatically learn hierarchical representations. CNNs have revolutionized image classification, object detection, and image generation tasks.

Recurrent Neural Networks: Recurrent neural networks (RNNs) are neural networks that can process sequential data by maintaining internal memory. RNNs allow information to persist across previous steps, making them suitable for tasks such as natural language processing, speech recognition, and time series analysis. Long Short-Term Memory (LSTM) and Gated Recurrent Units (GRUs) are popular types of RNNs that address the vanishing gradient problem.

Generative Adversarial Networks: Generative adversarial networks (GANs) are a type of deep learning model that consists of both a generator and a discriminator network. The generator network learns to generate synthetic data, such as images, while the discriminator network learns to distinguish between real and synthetic data. GANs have achieved impressive results in image synthesis, style transfer, and data augmentation.

Emerging Trends

The field of machine learning continues to evolve rapidly, with exciting new trends emerging. Here are some of the current areas of interest and research:

Transfer Learning: Transfer learning focuses on leveraging knowledge gained from one task or domain to improve performance on another related task or domain. By transferring learned representations or models, transfer learning enables effective learning with limited labeled data and accelerates the training process.

Explainable AI: As machine learning models become increasingly complex, interpreting and explaining their decisions becomes crucial. Explainable AI aims to provide insights into how models arrive at their decisions, addressing concerns regarding interpretability, fairness, and bias. This field explores techniques such as attention mechanisms, rule extraction, and model-agnostic explanations.

Federated Learning: Federated learning is a distributed learning paradigm that allows multiple devices or entities to collaboratively train a shared model without exchanging raw data. This approach preserves data privacy and reduces the need for centralized data storage. Federated learning has gained attention in applications involving sensitive data, such as healthcare and finance.

AutoML and Meta-Learning: Automated machine learning (AutoML) aims to automate the entire machine learning pipeline, from data preprocessing to model selection and hyperparameter optimization. Similarly, meta-learning focuses on automatically learning algorithms or strategies for model optimization and adaptation. These fields aim to make machine learning more accessible and reduce the burden of manual model selection and configuration.

Challenges and Future Directions

While machine learning has made significant progress, it still faces several challenges and open research questions. Some of the key challenges include:

Data Bias and Ethics: Machine learning models are susceptible to bias present in the training data, leading to unfair or discriminatory outcomes. Addressing bias and ensuring ethical machine learning practices are crucial for building fair and inclusive systems.

Interpretability and Trust: As machine learning models become more complex, understanding their decision-making processes becomes increasingly difficult. Developing methods to interpret and explain model predictions is essential for building trust and ensuring accountability.

Robustness and Adversarial Attacks: Machine learning models are vulnerable to adversarial attacks, where malicious entities intentionally manipulate input data to deceive the model. Developing robust models that are resistant to such attacks is an ongoing research challenge.

Scalability and Resource Efficiency: Deep learning models can be computationally expensive and require significant computational resources. The development of efficient algorithms and scalable architectures is crucial for deploying machine learning models on resource-constrained devices and in large-scale systems.

In conclusion, machine learning paradigms have evolved significantly over time, from traditional statistical approaches to the current dominance of deep learning. The field continues to advance rapidly, with emerging trends such as transfer learning, explainable AI, federated learning, and AutoML shaping the future of machine learning. However, challenges related to data bias, interpretability, robustness, and scalability need to be addressed to unlock the full potential of machine learning in various domains.

Expert Systems

MYCIN: AI in Medical Diagnosis

One of the most notable applications of artificial intelligence (AI) in the field of medicine is the MYCIN system. Developed in the 1970s, MYCIN was designed to provide expert-level assistance in the diagnosis and treatment of infectious diseases. It utilized the power of AI to analyze patient symptoms and medical data, providing recommendations for appropriate antibiotics and dosages.

The Need for MYCIN

Diagnosing and treating infectious diseases can be a complex task, requiring extensive knowledge of medical conditions, symptoms, and treatment options. Physicians often need to consider numerous factors and weigh the risks and benefits of different treatment approaches. Human experts in specific medical domains possess this knowledge and expertise, but their availability may be limited, and their opinions can vary. MYCIN aimed to provide consistent, accurate, and timely assistance in infectious disease diagnosis, particularly in areas lacking expert medical personnel.

Knowledge Representation in MYCIN

MYCIN represented medical knowledge using a rule-based expert system. It consisted of a knowledge base containing a set of rules and a rule engine that inferred conclusions based on these rules. The rules encoded the expertise of human clinicians, stating the conditions under which specific diagnoses and treatments would apply.

For example, a rule in the MYCIN knowledge base might state: "If the patient has a high fever, a positive blood culture, and a rapid pulse, and the blood culture shows the presence of Gram-negative bacteria, then diagnose the patient with sepsis."

Inference Engine and Uncertainty

The inference engine of MYCIN performed logical reasoning on the rules to reach diagnoses and treatment recommendations. It used a backward-chaining approach, starting with the goal (e.g., identifying the disease) and working backward through the rules to find the conditions that satisfied the goal.

One important aspect of MYCIN was its ability to handle uncertainty. Medical diagnosis often involves incomplete or uncertain information, and MYCIN incorporated uncertainty factors into its reasoning process. It used a probabilistic approach, assigning values to various factors based on the likelihood of their occurrence. For example, if there was uncertainty in the presence of a symptom, MYCIN would assign a probability value to consider its possible presence or absence.

MYCIN's Contributions and Limitations

MYCIN made significant contributions to the field of medical diagnosis. It demonstrated how AI techniques could be employed successfully to assist physicians in complex decision-making processes. It provided a systematic and consistent approach to diagnosing infectious diseases, reducing the reliance on human expertise alone.

However, MYCIN also had limitations. Its knowledge base was built on the expertise of a small group of clinicians, which could introduce biases and limit its generalizability. Additionally, the system's ability to handle uncertainty, while advanced for its time, still had limitations compared to the nuances of human intuition and judgment. MYCIN's success in medical diagnosis paved the way for further research and development in AI applications in healthcare.

Contemporary Applications

While MYCIN itself is no longer in active use, its legacy lives on in contemporary AI applications in medical diagnosis. Modern expert systems and machine learning algorithms have improved the accuracy and efficiency of diagnosing infectious diseases, as well as other medical conditions.

AI algorithms can now analyze vast amounts of medical data, including electronic health records, medical images, and genetic information. They can assist physicians in predicting patient outcomes, identifying potential drug interactions, and personalizing treatment plans. These advancements have the potential to greatly enhance healthcare delivery, improve patient outcomes, and alleviate the burden on medical professionals.

Ethical Considerations

As with any AI application in healthcare, ethical considerations surrounding data privacy, algorithmic bias, and patient autonomy are essential. AI systems must handle sensitive patient information with strict confidentiality and adhere to legal and ethical standards. Rigorous testing and validation processes are crucial to ensure the accuracy and reliability of AI algorithms in medical diagnosis. Additionally, clear communication between AI systems and healthcare providers is vital to maintain shared decision-making and respect patient autonomy.

Further Reading

For those interested in exploring the topic further, the following resources provide valuable insights into the MYCIN system and AI in medical diagnosis:

- Shortliffe, E. H. (2006). "MYCIN: A retrospect." Artificial Intelligence in Medicine, 38(3), 215-225.
- Szolovits, P. (2010). "Artificial intelligence in medicine." In Shortliffe, E. H., and Cimino, J. J. (Eds.), Biomedical Informatics: Computer Applications in Healthcare and Biomedicine (pp. 339-381). Springer.
- Ball, M. J., and Collen, M. F. (1991). "MYCIN to HELP: Evolutionary Changes in Decision Support Systems." In Collen, M. F., et al. (Eds.), A History of Medical Informatics in the United States, 1950 to 1990 (pp. 357-378). American Medical Informatics Association.

Summary

The MYCIN system was a pioneering AI application in medical diagnosis. By utilizing a rule-based expert system and addressing uncertainty, MYCIN provided valuable assistance to physicians in diagnosing infectious diseases. While advancements in AI have since surpassed MYCIN, its legacy remains in the development of contemporary AI algorithms and expert systems for medical diagnosis. Ethical considerations surrounding privacy, bias, and patient autonomy are crucial in the implementation of AI systems in healthcare.

Rule-Based Expert Systems

Rule-based expert systems are a type of artificial intelligence (AI) system designed to mimic the decision-making abilities of human experts in a particular domain. These systems are built using a set of rules or logical statements that encode the knowledge and expertise of the domain experts. Rule-based expert systems have been widely used in various fields, including medicine, engineering, finance, and manufacturing, to provide expert-level advice and decision support.

Principles of Rule-Based Expert Systems

The principles behind rule-based expert systems are rooted in symbolic AI, which focuses on representing knowledge and reasoning using symbols and rules. The key components of a rule-based expert system include:

1. Knowledge Base: The knowledge base contains a set of rules that represent the domain-specific knowledge and expertise. Each rule consists of an antecedent (if-part) and a consequent (then-part). The antecedent specifies the conditions that must be satisfied for the rule to be applicable, while the consequent defines the actions or conclusions to be taken when the rule is triggered.

2. Inference Engine: The inference engine is responsible for processing the rules in the knowledge base and deriving conclusions or making recommendations based on the available information. It uses a variety of reasoning mechanisms, such as forward chaining (data-driven reasoning) or backward chaining (goal-driven reasoning), to infer new facts or make decisions.

3. User Interface: The user interface provides a means for users to interact with the expert system. It allows users to

input their specific problem or question and receive advice or recommendations based on the system's knowledge and reasoning.

4. Explanation Mechanism: Rule-based expert systems often include an explanation mechanism that provides justification or reasoning behind the system's responses. This mechanism helps users understand how the system arrived at a particular conclusion and builds trust and confidence in the system.

Rule-Based Expert Systems in Practice

To illustrate the practical application of rule-based expert systems, let's consider a medical diagnosis system for skin diseases. The knowledge base of the expert system contains rules that capture the symptoms and relationships between different skin diseases. Here are a few example rules:

```
IF patient\index{patient} has a\index{a} rash\index{ra
IF patient\index{patient} has a\index{a} rash\index{ra
IF patient\index{patient} has a\index{a} rash\index{ra
```

In this example, the antecedent of each rule describes a specific symptom or condition, and the consequent suggests a potential diagnosis based on the presence of that symptom. The inference engine of the expert system evaluates the rules based on the patient's symptoms and derives the appropriate diagnosis.

When a user interacts with the system, they can input their symptoms, such as rash, itchiness, and pain. The inference engine matches these inputs with the antecedents of the rules in the knowledge base and triggers the corresponding rules. Based on the triggered rules, the system generates a diagnosis or a list of potential diagnoses.

To provide an explanation for the diagnosis, the expert system can explain the rules that were triggered and the specific symptoms that led to the conclusion. This helps the user understand why certain diagnoses were suggested and enables them to ask further questions or seek additional clarification.

Advantages and Limitations of Rule-Based Expert Systems

Rule-based expert systems offer several advantages compared to traditional decision-making approaches:

- **Rapid Decision-Making:** Expert systems can analyze a vast amount of information and apply complex reasoning in a short amount of time, enabling quick and accurate decision-making.
- **Consistency and Reliability:** Expert systems provide consistent and reliable advice based on established rules and domain expertise. They are not influenced by emotions or external factors that may affect human decision-making.
- **Knowledge Preservation:** Rule-based expert systems allow the knowledge and expertise of domain experts to be captured and preserved, even after their retirement or absence.

However, rule-based expert systems also have limitations:

- **Limited Adaptability:** Rule-based systems rely on predefined rules and may struggle with new or unusual situations that are not covered by the existing rules.
- **Inability to Handle Uncertainty:** Rule-based systems struggle with uncertain or incomplete information, as they

require precise conditions to trigger the rules. Dealing with uncertain or ambiguous data may lead to inaccurate or incomplete results.

- **Subjectivity in Rule Creation:** Developing the rules for an expert system often requires input from human experts, which introduces subjectivity and the potential for biases or errors.

Real-World Applications

Rule-based expert systems have been successfully applied in various domains. Here are a few examples:

- **Medical Diagnosis:** Expert systems have been developed to assist healthcare professionals in diagnosing diseases, interpreting medical images, and recommending treatment plans.
- **Financial Planning:** Rule-based systems have been used to provide personalized investment advice based on the client's financial goals, risk tolerance, and market conditions.
- **Quality Control:** Expert systems have been utilized in manufacturing industries to monitor production processes, detect anomalies or defects, and suggest corrective actions.
- **Troubleshooting and Maintenance:** Rule-based systems have been employed to guide users or technicians in troubleshooting equipment malfunctions or performing maintenance tasks.

Challenges and Future Directions

While rule-based expert systems have proven to be valuable tools, there are several challenges and future directions for improvement:

- **Integrating Machine Learning:** Combining rule-based systems with machine learning techniques can enhance their adaptability and ability to handle uncertainty. Machine learning algorithms can learn from historical data and make recommendations or update the rules based on patterns and trends.

- **Explainability and Transparency:** As expert systems are used in sensitive domains, such as healthcare and finance, it is crucial to make their reasoning transparent and explainable. Developing methods to explain the system's decision-making process can foster trust and acceptance from users.

- **Collaborative Expert Systems:** Building expert systems that can collaborate with human experts can leverage the collective intelligence and domain expertise. These systems can work in tandem with human experts to provide comprehensive and accurate advice.

In summary, rule-based expert systems provide a powerful means of capturing and utilizing domain expertise to make intelligent decisions and provide expert-level advice. While they have their limitations, continuous advancements in AI and machine learning present exciting opportunities for enhancing the capabilities of rule-based expert systems and expanding their applications in various domains.

Knowledge Representation in AI

Knowledge representation is a fundamental aspect of artificial intelligence (AI) that deals with the representation, organization, and manipulation of knowledge within a computer system. It provides a way for AI systems to store and reason with knowledge, enabling them to make informed decisions and solve complex problems.

Introduction to Knowledge Representation

In AI, knowledge representation involves selecting appropriate structures and formats to represent knowledge in a machine-readable form. The choice of representation affects the efficiency and effectiveness of AI systems in reasoning, learning, and problem-solving tasks.

The aim of knowledge representation in AI is to capture the semantics of the real-world domain being modeled. Different AI systems may use different representations depending on the nature of the problem and the application domain. Some common forms of knowledge representation include logical representations, semantic networks, frames, and ontologies.

Logical Representations

Logical representations in AI use formal logic to represent and reason with knowledge. Propositional logic and first-order logic are commonly used for knowledge representation, allowing AI systems to express statements about the world and manipulate them using logical rules.

Propositional logic represents knowledge in propositional sentences or statements. It uses logical operators such as AND, OR, and NOT to combine atomic propositions and form more complex statements. For example, the statement "It is raining AND the ground is wet" can be represented as:

$$Rain \wedge WetGround$$

First-order logic extends propositional logic by introducing variables, quantifiers, and predicates to represent more complex knowledge. Predicates represent relationships between objects, while quantifiers specify the scope of variables. For example, the statement "All cats are mammals" can be represented in first-order logic as:

$$\forall x, Cat(x) \implies Mammal(x)$$

Logical representations provide a solid foundation for knowledge representation in AI, allowing for precise and formal reasoning. However, they can be limited in representing uncertain or probabilistic knowledge.

Semantic Networks

Semantic networks represent knowledge as a network of interconnected nodes, where each node represents a concept or an object, and the edges represent relationships between them. Concepts and relationships are typically represented using natural language labels or symbols.

For example, consider a semantic network representing knowledge about animals. Each node in the network could represent an animal, and the edges between nodes could represent relationships such as "is a" (e.g., "cat is a mammal") or "eats" (e.g., "lion eats meat").

Semantic networks are useful for representing hierarchical relationships, taxonomies, and general knowledge structures. They provide a graphical representation that is intuitive and easily interpretable by humans. However, they can become complex and unwieldy for large knowledge bases.

Frames

Frames are a form of knowledge representation that organizes knowledge into structured units called frames. Each frame represents a concept or an object and contains attributes that describe its properties and relationships with other concepts.

A frame consists of slots, which store values for specific attributes of the concept or object. Slots can be basic types (e.g., strings, numbers) or complex types (e.g., other frames or lists of frames). For example, a frame representing a car could have slots for attributes such as "model," "color," and "manufacturer."

Frames provide a flexible and extensible representation for knowledge, allowing for the definition of inheritance hierarchies, default values, and procedural attachments. They are particularly suitable for representing structured knowledge domains where objects have well-defined properties and relationships.

Ontologies

Ontologies are a formalized representation of knowledge that defines a set of concepts and the relationships between them within a specific domain. They provide a shared vocabulary for describing a domain and enable interoperability between different AI systems and applications.

Ontologies are often represented using the Web Ontology Language (OWL) or similar formal languages. They consist of classes, properties, and individuals. Classes represent concepts or categories, properties represent relationships between concepts, and individuals represent specific instances of concepts.

The use of ontologies in knowledge representation allows for semantic interoperability, enables automated reasoning, and supports intelligent searching and querying of knowledge bases. Ontologies are commonly used in fields such as bioinformatics, e-commerce, and semantic web applications.

Knowledge Representation in Practice

In practice, knowledge representation in AI involves selecting the most appropriate representation scheme based on the problem domain and the requirements of the AI system. Often, a combination of different representation schemes is used to capture the nuances and complexities of real-world knowledge.

The choice of knowledge representation impacts the efficiency and effectiveness of AI systems in various tasks, such as problem-solving, decision-making, natural language processing, and knowledge discovery. It affects the system's ability to represent and reason with uncertainty, handle incomplete or inconsistent information, and learn from new knowledge.

For example, in a medical diagnosis system, knowledge about diseases, symptoms, and treatments can be represented using frames or ontologies. The system can use logical rules to reason about symptoms and infer possible diseases based on the available evidence. It can also employ probabilistic models to handle uncertain or missing information.

Conclusion

Knowledge representation is a crucial aspect of AI systems, enabling them to store, reason with, and manipulate knowledge. Logical representations, semantic networks, frames, and ontologies are commonly used schemes for representing knowledge in AI. Each scheme has its strengths and limitations, and the choice of representation depends on the nature of the problem and the application domain.

Effective knowledge representation allows AI systems to make intelligent decisions, solve complex problems, and learn from new information. It forms the foundation for many AI applications and plays a vital role in shaping the future of AI technology.

Further reading:

- Brachman, R.J., & Levesque, H.J. (2004). Knowledge Representation and Reasoning. Morgan Kaufmann. - Russell, S., & Norvig, P. (2016). Artificial Intelligence: A Modern Approach. Pearson. - Genesereth, M.R., & Nilsson, N.J. (1987). Logical Foundations of Artificial Intelligence. Morgan

Kaufmann. - Gruber, T.R. (1993). A Translation Approach to Portable Ontology Specifications. Knowledge Acquisition, 5(2), 199-220.

Quantum Computing

Quantum Mechanics and Computing

Quantum Bits (Qubits)

In the field of quantum computing, the basic unit of information is called a *quantum bit*, or *qubit*. While classical computing uses bits that can represent either a 0 or a 1, qubits have the unique ability to exist in a state of superposition, simultaneously representing 0 and 1. This property gives qubits the potential to perform computations exponentially faster than classical bits.

Background

To understand the concept of qubits, we need to briefly explore the principles of quantum mechanics. Quantum mechanics describes the behavior of particles at the smallest scales, such as atoms and subatomic particles. One of the key principles of quantum mechanics is superposition, which states that a particle can exist in multiple states simultaneously.

In classical computing, we use bits to store and process information. A bit can take on one of two values: 0 or 1. In contrast, a qubit can be in a superposition of 0 and 1, represented by a complex mathematical expression known as a wavefunction.

The wavefunction gives the probability amplitudes for the qubit to be measured in the states 0 or 1.

Mathematical Representation

The state of a qubit can be represented using Dirac notation, a mathematical notation commonly used in quantum mechanics. A qubit in a state of superposition can be expressed as:

$$|\psi\rangle = \alpha\,|0\rangle + \beta\,|1\rangle$$

where α and β are complex probability amplitudes, satisfying the normalization condition $|\alpha|^2 + |\beta|^2 = 1$. The probability of measuring the qubit in state $|0\rangle$ is $|\alpha|^2$, and the probability of measuring it in state $|1\rangle$ is $|\beta|^2$.

The complex probability amplitudes α and β contain both magnitude and phase information, allowing qubits to exhibit interference phenomena. This interference is at the heart of many quantum algorithms and computational advantages.

Quantum Gates

Just like classical bits can be manipulated using logic gates, qubits can be manipulated using quantum gates. Quantum gates are represented by unitary matrices that operate on the qubits' wavefunctions. These gates can change the probability amplitudes and, consequently, the state of the qubit.

Some common quantum gates include the Hadamard gate (H), the Pauli gates (X, Y, and Z), and the phase gate (S). These gates enable operations such as creating superposition, flipping the qubit between 0 and 1, and introducing phase shifts.

By combining multiple quantum gates, complex transformations can be applied to qubits, allowing for the implementation of various quantum algorithms.

Entanglement

Another crucial property of qubits is entanglement. When two or more qubits become entangled, their states become correlated in such a way that the state of one qubit cannot be described independently of the other(s).

Entangled qubits exhibit a phenomenon called *quantum entanglement*, where manipulating the state of one qubit instantly affects the state of the other, regardless of the distance between them. This non-local correlation is one of the most fascinating aspects of quantum computing and holds significant potential for applications such as secure communication and quantum teleportation.

Real-world Challenges and Limitations

While qubits offer great promise, harnessing their power is not without challenges. Some of the main hurdles of working with qubits include:

1. **Decoherence:** Qubits are highly sensitive to interactions with their environment, leading to a loss of coherence known as decoherence. Decoherence causes the wavefunction to collapse and introduces errors in computations. Efforts are being made to mitigate decoherence and improve qubit stability.

2. **Error Correction:** Errors due to decoherence and other sources pose a significant problem in quantum computing. Developing error-correcting codes and fault-tolerant quantum systems is a critical area of research.

3. **Scalability:** Building large-scale quantum computers that can perform complex computations remains a significant challenge. Increasing the number of qubits in a system

while maintaining their coherence and minimizing error rates is an ongoing endeavor.

Despite these challenges, quantum bits (qubits) hold tremendous potential for revolutionizing computational power and tackling problems that are computationally infeasible with classical computers.

Resources

For further exploration of the topic, we recommend the following resources:

- *Quantum Computing for Computer Scientists* by Yanofsky and Mannucci: This book provides a comprehensive introduction to quantum computing, covering topics from basic principles to quantum algorithms and applications.
- *Quantum Computing: A Gentle Introduction* by Eleanor G. Rieffel and Wolfgang H. Polak: This book offers an accessible introduction to the field of quantum computing, suitable for readers with no prior background in quantum mechanics.
- IBM Quantum Experience: IBM provides a cloud-based platform for experimenting with quantum computing. Their website offers learning resources, tutorials, and access to real quantum systems for hands-on exploration.

With these resources and a deeper understanding of qubits, you are now prepared to delve into the exciting world of quantum computing.

Superposition and Entanglement

In the previous section, we explored the principles of quantum mechanics and their relevance to computing. One of the most fascinating and fundamental concepts in quantum computing is superposition, which allows quantum bits (qubits) to exist in multiple states simultaneously. Alongside superposition, another key concept is entanglement, where qubits become interconnected in a way that their states are correlated, regardless of the physical distance between them. In this section, we will delve deeper into superposition and entanglement and their implications for quantum computing.

Superposition: The Power of Multiple States

Superposition is at the heart of quantum computing's potential for exponential computational power. While classical bits can only represent states as either 0 or 1, qubits can exist in a superposition of both states simultaneously. This means that a qubit can be in a linear combination of the basis states $|0\boxtimes$ and $|1\boxtimes$, represented mathematically as:

$$|\psi\boxtimes = \alpha|0\boxtimes + \beta|1\boxtimes$$

Here, ⊠ and ⊠ are complex numbers known as probability amplitudes, which determine the probability of measuring the qubit in either state $|0\boxtimes$ or $|1\boxtimes$. The probabilities are given by the square of the absolute values of the probability amplitudes: $||^2$ and $||^2$. Importantly, $||^2 + ||^2$ must equal 1, ensuring that the probability of finding a qubit in one of the basis states is 100%.

To illustrate the concept of superposition, let's consider an example. Suppose we have a qubit in the state:

$$|\psi\boxtimes = \frac{1}{\sqrt{2}}|0\boxtimes + \frac{1}{\sqrt{2}}|1\boxtimes$$

When this qubit is measured, there is an equal probability of obtaining either 0 or 1. However, before measurement, the qubit exists in a superposition of both states simultaneously, providing a parallelism not found in classical computing.

Entanglement: Spooky Action at a Distance

Entanglement is another remarkable phenomenon in quantum mechanics that plays a crucial role in quantum computing. When two or more qubits become entangled, their states become intertwined in a way that the state of one qubit cannot be described independently of the others.

Consider a system of two qubits, qubit A and qubit B. If the two qubits are entangled, the combined state of the system cannot be represented as a simple product of the individual qubit states. Instead, the entangled state is represented as:

$$|\phi\rangle = \alpha|00\rangle + \beta|01\rangle + \gamma|10\rangle + \delta|11\rangle$$

Here, ⊠, ⊠, ⊠, and ⊠ are probability amplitudes. Notably, the state of each qubit, when measured individually, is indeterminate. It is only when the qubits are measured together that their states are revealed.

The implications of entanglement are far-reaching. Entangled qubits can be used to transmit information instantaneously over large distances, defying the constraints of classical physics. This property is often referred to as "spooky action at a distance," as famously described by Albert Einstein. Furthermore, entanglement enables quantum computers to perform certain computations exponentially faster than classical computers, making it a fundamental resource for quantum algorithms.

Applications and Challenges

Superposition and entanglement offer exciting possibilities for quantum computing. They facilitate parallel processing, giving quantum computers the potential to solve complex problems much faster than classical computers. Furthermore, entanglement allows for the creation of highly secure cryptographic systems and the simulation of quantum systems that are computationally intractable for classical computers.

However, harnessing the power of superposition and entanglement is not without its challenges. Environmental noise and interference can cause qubits to lose their quantum nature, leading to errors in computations. This phenomenon is known as decoherence. Overcoming decoherence is a major hurdle in the development of practical quantum computers and requires robust error correction techniques and advanced quantum control methods.

Another challenge is the difficulty of creating and maintaining entanglement between multiple qubits, especially as the number of qubits in a system increases. As the complexity of entangled states grows exponentially with the number of qubits, the resources and control required to manipulate them become increasingly demanding.

Conclusion

Superposition and entanglement are foundational principles in quantum computing that enable the harnessing of quantum effects for computational purposes. Superposition allows qubits to exist in multiple states simultaneously, opening up the potential for exponential parallelism. Entanglement, on the other hand, connects qubits in a way that their states become correlated, enabling the transmission of information and facilitating powerful quantum algorithms.

While superposition and entanglement offer exciting opportunities for quantum computing, the challenges of maintaining coherence and scaling up entanglement pose significant obstacles. Overcoming these challenges is critical for realizing the full potential of quantum computing and exploring new frontiers in computation and information processing.

In the next section, we will explore the intriguing field of quantum algorithms and their potential to solve complex problems that are intractable for classical computers.

Quantum Computers: A New Frontier

IBM Quantum Computers

In this section, we will explore the advancements in quantum computing made by IBM. Quantum computing is an exciting and rapidly evolving field that leverages the principles of quantum mechanics to perform calculations exponentially faster than classical computers. IBM has been at the forefront of quantum computing research and development, pushing the boundaries of what is possible in this field.

Introduction to Quantum Computing

Before delving into IBM's contributions, let's briefly review the principles of quantum computing. In classical computing, information is stored in bits, which can take on a value of either 0 or 1. Quantum computing, on the other hand, uses quantum bits or qubits, which can exist in a superposition of states, representing both 0 and 1 simultaneously. This unique property of qubits enables quantum computers to perform parallel computations and solve certain types of problems much faster than classical computers.

IBM Quantum Experience (QX)

IBM Quantum Experience (QX) is a cloud-based platform that allows researchers, developers, and enthusiasts to access and experiment with quantum computers developed by IBM. It provides a user-friendly interface and a set of tools for designing and executing quantum computations.

IBM Quantum Processors

IBM has made significant advancements in developing scalable and reliable quantum processors. The IBM Q System One is a quantum computer designed for commercial use, featuring 20 qubits and a stable, cryogenic environment. IBM is continuously working on increasing the number of qubits and improving the overall performance of their quantum processors.

Qiskit: IBM's Quantum Software Framework

To facilitate programming and experimentation with quantum computers, IBM has developed Qiskit, an open-source quantum software framework. Qiskit provides a comprehensive suite of tools and libraries for working with quantum circuits, running simulations, and interfacing with real quantum hardware.

Applications of IBM Quantum Computers

IBM's quantum computers have shown promising potential for solving complex problems in various domains. Here are a few notable applications:

- **Cryptography:** Quantum computers have the potential to break current encryption algorithms, but they can also be used to develop quantum-safe cryptographic techniques.

- **Optimization and Simulation:** Quantum algorithms can be used to solve optimization problems, such as finding the most efficient routes for logistics or maximizing portfolio returns. Quantum simulation can also provide insights into the behavior of complex systems, such as chemical reactions or materials science.

- **Machine Learning:** Quantum computers can enhance machine learning algorithms by efficiently processing and analyzing large datasets. They can also accelerate training processes and enable the exploration of novel machine learning models designed specifically for quantum hardware.

- **Quantum Chemistry and Material Science:** The simulation of quantum systems is a natural fit for quantum computers. They can be used to simulate molecular properties, catalytic reactions, and the behavior of materials at the atomic level, which can lead to the discovery of new drugs, catalysts, and materials.

Current Challenges and Future Directions

Although IBM has made remarkable progress in quantum computing, several challenges remain to be addressed. Some key challenges include:

- **Quantum Error Correction:** Quantum systems are highly susceptible to errors caused by noise and decoherence. Implementing robust error correction techniques is crucial for preserving the integrity of quantum computations.

- **Scaling Up:** Building larger, more powerful quantum computers with a higher number of qubits and lower error rates is essential for tackling more complex problems.

- **Algorithm Development:** Developing and optimizing algorithms specifically designed for quantum hardware is crucial for unlocking the full potential of quantum computers.

- **Integration with Classical Computing:** Quantum computers are not intended to replace classical computers but rather to complement them. Developing efficient methods for integrating classical and quantum computing systems will be vital for realizing practical applications.

Looking ahead, IBM and the quantum computing community are committed to addressing these challenges and continue pushing the boundaries of quantum computing. The future of quantum computing holds tremendous opportunities and transformative potential across various industries and scientific disciplines.

Conclusion

IBM's contributions to quantum computing have been instrumental in advancing the field. With their cloud-based quantum computing platform, IBM Quantum Experience, and their constant efforts to improve quantum processors and develop advanced algorithms, they have played a significant role in bringing quantum computing closer to reality. As the field continues to evolve, IBM remains at the forefront of research, innovation, and the exploration of new applications for quantum computers.

Further Reading

For those interested in diving deeper into the world of IBM quantum computers, here are some recommended resources:

1. IBM Quantum Experience: `https://www.ibm.com/quantum-computing`
2. Qiskit Documentation: `https://qiskit.org/documentation/`
3. "Quantum Computing for Computer Scientists" by Noson S. Yanofsky and Mirco A. Mannucci
4. "Quantum Computing: An Applied Approach" by Jack D. Hidary

These resources provide a wealth of information about the principles, applications, and practical aspects of quantum computing, as well as hands-on guides for programming quantum computers using Qiskit. Happy quantum computing exploration!

Google's Quantum Supremacy Claim

In recent years, quantum computing has emerged as a promising field that has the potential to revolutionize the way we solve complex problems. One significant milestone in the field occurred in 2019 when Google made a startling announcement - they had achieved quantum supremacy. But what exactly does this mean?

Background

To understand Google's claim, we need to first grasp the concept of quantum supremacy. Quantum supremacy refers to the point at which a quantum computer can solve a problem that is beyond the capabilities of the most powerful classical supercomputers. In other words, it is the ability of a quantum computer to perform calculations that are infeasible for classical computers to accomplish in a reasonable amount of time.

The Experiment

To demonstrate quantum supremacy, Google introduced a quantum processor called Sycamore, comprising 54 qubits - the essential building blocks of quantum computing. They set out to solve a specific problem - the sampling task, which involves generating random numbers following a specific distribution.

The classical counterpart to this quantum sampling task is computationally expensive, even for the most powerful supercomputers. Google's claim was that Sycamore could perform this task significantly faster than any classical computer.

The Results

Google's team, led by John Martinis, stated that their quantum processor achieved the sampling task in just 200 seconds, a time frame that classical computers would require thousands of years to match. This groundbreaking result effectively demonstrated their claim of quantum supremacy.

Controversy and Challenges

While Google's claim was met with excitement and enthusiasm within the quantum computing community, it also generated skepticism and debate. Some researchers questioned whether the task tackled by Sycamore was truly a relevant problem or if it was purely a contrived case designed to showcase quantum supremacy.

Additionally, the quantum processor used in the experiment was extremely error-prone, with high error rates in qubit operations and measurements. Critics argued that this limited the practical utility of the achievement since error correction techniques will be necessary for quantum computers to be genuinely useful.

Implications and Future Directions

Google's quantum supremacy claim marks a significant milestone in the development of quantum computing. It demonstrates that quantum computers have the potential to surpass classical computers in certain computations, even with current error rates.

The achievement opens up new avenues for exploration and research in quantum algorithms, optimization problems, cryptography, and material simulations. It also motivates further investment and development in error correction techniques to improve the reliability and scalability of quantum processors.

While Google's claim has been debated, it serves as a catalyst for both collaboration and competition within the field of quantum computing. Other major players, such as IBM and Microsoft, have redoubled their efforts to push the boundaries of quantum technology, ensuring that this remarkable milestone is only the beginning of a new era in computing.

Conclusion

Google's claim of achieving quantum supremacy with their Sycamore quantum processor has ignited excitement and debate within the scientific community. While the achievement is undoubtedly significant, it also raises important questions about the practical utility and scalability of quantum computing.

As researchers continue to refine quantum hardware and develop new algorithms, we can expect ongoing advancements that bring us closer to realizing the full potential of quantum computing. The path forward is filled with challenges, but the rewards could revolutionize not only the field of computing but also our understanding of the universe.

Challenges in Quantum Computing

Quantum computing is a rapidly advancing field with the potential to revolutionize various aspects of technology and science. However, like any emerging technology, it faces several challenges that need to be overcome to realize its full potential. In this section, we will explore some of the key challenges in the field of quantum computing and discuss the current research and solutions being pursued.

Physical Implementation

One of the fundamental challenges in quantum computing is the physical implementation of qubits, the basic units of quantum information. Qubits are fragile and susceptible to environmental noise, such as electromagnetic interference and temperature fluctuations. These disturbances can cause errors in the qubit state, leading to incorrect computation results. In order to build scalable and reliable quantum computers, it is crucial to develop qubits with longer coherence times and high-fidelity operations.

Researchers are exploring various physical systems for qubit implementation, such as superconducting circuits, trapped ions, topological qubits, and spin qubits. Each of these platforms has its own advantages and challenges. For example, superconducting qubits have shown promise in terms of scalability and fast gate operations, but they also require extremely low temperatures and strict control over electromagnetic fields. Trapped ion qubits, on the other hand, have long coherence times but face challenges in achieving high-speed operations.

Quantum Error Correction

Quantum error correction is a vital aspect of building reliable quantum computers. Due to the inherent noise in quantum systems, errors can occur during computational operations.

Unlike classical computers, where errors can be corrected by duplicating information and performing redundancy checks, quantum error correction is more complex due to the no-cloning theorem.

Quantum error correction codes are designed to detect and correct errors in qubits by encoding multiple qubits into a highly entangled state known as an error-correcting code. However, implementing these codes requires a significant overhead in terms of qubit resources and computational operations. Furthermore, errors in the error correction process can propagate and accumulate, leading to the failure of error correction itself.

Researchers are actively developing and optimizing quantum error correction codes to mitigate these challenges. The goal is to find codes that can correct a reasonable number of errors while minimizing resource overhead.

Quantum Gates and Circuit Optimization

In classical computing, logic gates are used to manipulate bits and perform computations. Similarly, in quantum computing, quantum gates are applied to qubits to perform quantum operations. However, designing and optimizing quantum gates and circuits is a challenging task.

Quantum gates need to be accurate, have low gate errors, and operate within a given time constraint. Achieving these requirements becomes increasingly difficult as the number of qubits and gates in a quantum circuit increases. Additionally, the optimization of quantum circuits to reduce gate count and increase efficiency is a non-trivial problem.

Researchers are developing novel techniques and algorithms for designing and optimizing quantum gates and circuits. These include compiling high-level quantum programs into low-level gate sequences, developing efficient gate libraries, and exploring hardware-specific optimizations. Additionally, machine learning approaches are being applied to improve gate fidelity and circuit performance.

Quantum Decoherence

Quantum decoherence is a phenomenon where quantum systems lose their coherence and become entangled with the surrounding environment. This loss of coherence leads to the degradation of quantum information, making it difficult to perform precise quantum operations and maintain the stability of qubits.

Various sources contribute to quantum decoherence, including interaction with environmental noise, imperfections in qubit control, and coupling between qubits. To mitigate quantum decoherence, researchers are exploring techniques such as error correction codes, quantum error avoidance, and dynamical decoupling. These methods aim to minimize the impact of decoherence and extend the coherence times of qubits.

Scaling and Connectivity

Scalability is a critical challenge in quantum computing. Building a quantum computer with a large number of qubits and maintaining the connectivity between them is essential for solving complex problems. However, as the number of qubits increases, the challenges of fabrication, control, and maintaining coherence become more significant.

Another challenge is achieving long-range connectivity between qubits. In current quantum systems, qubits are typically arranged in a local connectivity pattern, limiting the types of algorithms that can be efficiently executed. To overcome this challenge, researchers are exploring the use of distributed architectures, such as qubit arrays and modular systems, to achieve scalable and long-range qubit connectivity.

Quantum Software and Algorithm Development

While significant progress has been made in hardware development, quantum software and algorithm development play a crucial role in realizing the potential of quantum computing. Designing quantum algorithms that can efficiently solve complex problems and mapping them onto physical quantum hardware present a significant challenge.

Quantum algorithms often require careful consideration of qubit connectivity, gate count, gate errors, and noise characteristics. Developing and optimizing quantum software for a diverse range of applications, such as optimization problems, cryptography, and simulation, requires new programming paradigms and tools.

Researchers are actively working on developing quantum programming languages, software libraries, and compilers to bridge the gap between quantum algorithms and physical hardware. These tools aim to make quantum programming more accessible and enable the development of efficient and robust quantum algorithms.

Conclusion

Quantum computing holds tremendous promise for solving complex problems that are beyond the reach of classical computers. However, numerous challenges need to be overcome to realize the full potential of this technology. From physical implementation and error correction to software development and scalability, researchers around the world are actively working towards addressing these challenges.

While significant progress has been made, there is still much to be done before quantum computers become practical and widely available. As quantum computing continues to evolve, it is expected to reshape industries, accelerate scientific discoveries, and bring about new computational capabilities that were once thought to be impossible. The challenges we discussed in this section are not meant to discourage progress but to highlight the areas that require further exploration and innovation. Quantum computing is at the forefront of a new era of computation, and the solutions to these challenges will pave the way for future breakthroughs.

Ethical and Social Implications

Privacy Concerns

Data Collection and Surveillance

In the digital age, data has become an invaluable resource. From personal information to user preferences, a vast amount of data is collected and stored by various entities. Data collection can have significant benefits, such as improving services and tailoring experiences to individual needs. However, it also raises concerns about privacy and surveillance. In this section, we will explore the topic of data collection and surveillance, examining the challenges and ethical implications involved.

Types of Data Collection

Data collection can occur in various ways, including but not limited to:

- **Passive data collection:** This type of data collection is carried out without the active participation or knowledge of the individuals involved. It often involves the gathering of data through online tracking mechanisms, such as cookies, and the monitoring of user behavior on websites and apps.

- **Active data collection:** Active data collection occurs when individuals willingly provide their data through surveys, questionnaires, or social media platforms. This may include personal information, preferences, or opinions.

- **Sensor-based data collection:** With the proliferation of Internet of Things (IoT) devices, data can now be collected through sensors embedded in various objects, such as smartwatches or home automation systems. These sensors can track physical activities, location, or environmental conditions.

Methods and Techniques

To collect and process large amounts of data efficiently, organizations employ various methods and techniques. Some common approaches include:

- **Big Data Analytics:** Organizations use algorithms and statistical models to analyze large datasets, looking for patterns and trends that can be used to make informed decisions. Data mining, machine learning, and natural language processing are some techniques used in big data analytics.

- **Social Network Analysis:** By analyzing social connections, interactions, and behavior on platforms such as Facebook and Twitter, researchers can identify influential individuals, communities, and sentiments. Social network analysis plays a vital role in marketing, politics, and security.

- **Video and Image Recognition:** Advanced computer vision techniques allow the extraction and analysis of information from images and videos. Facial recognition, object detection, and image classification are examples of image recognition technologies used in law enforcement, marketing, and surveillance systems.

Ethical Implications

Data collection and surveillance raise significant ethical concerns. Here are a few key considerations:

1. **Privacy:** The collection and storage of personal data can infringe upon individual privacy. Without proper safeguards, individuals may not have control over how their data is used or shared. Privacy laws and regulations, such as the General Data Protection Regulation (GDPR) in the European Union, have been implemented to protect individuals' privacy rights.

2. **Informed Consent:** Individuals have the right to be aware of what data is being collected, how it is being used, and who has access to it. Obtaining informed consent ensures that individuals have a choice in sharing their data and can make informed decisions.

3. **Data Security:** Protecting collected data from unauthorized access and breaches is crucial. Organizations must implement robust security measures, including encryption, access controls, and employee training, to safeguard sensitive information.

4. **Surveillance and Monitoring:** Surveillance activities raise concerns about the balance between public safety and individual privacy. The proliferation of surveillance cameras, facial recognition technology, and data analysis tools has sparked debates over the extent of surveillance in society.

Case Study: Online Advertising and Personalization

One area where data collection and surveillance have significant implications is online advertising. Companies collect user data to deliver targeted ads based on individuals' interests and preferences. While personalized ads can improve user experience and help advertisers reach their target audience, they also raise ethical concerns.

Consider the following example: Sarah, a social media user, frequently searches for healthy recipes and follows fitness influencers. Sarah's data is collected and analyzed, and she starts seeing advertisements for fitness gear and organic food products. On one hand, these tailored ads may genuinely interest Sarah and provide her with valuable information. On the other hand, she may feel that her personal space is being intruded upon and her privacy compromised.

One solution to this ethical dilemma is the concept of *opt-in* advertising, where users actively consent to sharing their data for personalized advertising. By giving users control over their data and providing transparency, organizations can strike a balance between personalization and privacy.

Protecting Personal Data

Individuals can take steps to protect their personal data in an era of pervasive data collection and surveillance. Here are some suggested methods:

- **Strong Passwords:** Using strong, unique passwords for online accounts helps prevent unauthorized access to personal information. Enabling two-factor authentication adds an extra layer of security.

- **Privacy Settings:** Review the privacy settings on social media platforms and adjust them to limit the visibility of personal information. Be mindful of what information is shared publicly, as it can be used for targeted advertising or other purposes.

- **Virtual Private Networks (VPNs):** VPNs encrypt internet traffic, providing a secure connection and protecting data from potential eavesdropping. They are particularly useful when using public Wi-Fi networks.

- **Avoiding Suspicious Links:** Phishing attacks often trick users into clicking on malicious links. Being cautious and verifying the legitimacy of links before clicking can help protect against malware and data breaches.

- **Regular Software Updates:** Keeping software and devices up-to-date with the latest security patches helps protect against known vulnerabilities and exploits.

Conclusion

Data collection and surveillance have become an integral part of our digital society. While they offer benefits such as improved services and personalization, they also raise important ethical concerns related to privacy, consent, and security. Striking a balance between data collection and privacy rights is crucial to ensure the responsible and ethical use of personal data. As technology continues to evolve, it is essential to remain vigilant and proactive in protecting our personal information and demanding transparency from organizations that collect and use our data.

References:

1. Mayer-Schönberger, Viktor, and Kenneth Cukier. "Big Data: A Revolution That Will Transform How We Live, Work, and Think." Houghton Mifflin Harcourt, 2013.

2. boyd, danah, and Kate Crawford. "Critical Questions for Big Data: Provocations for a Cultural, Technological, and Scholarly Phenomenon." Information, Communication & Society, vol. 15, no. 5, 2012, pp. 662-679.

3. Zuboff, Shoshana. "The Age of Surveillance Capitalism: The Fight for a Human Future at the New Frontier of Power." PublicAffairs, 2019.

4. O'Neil, Cathy. "Weapons of Math Destruction: How Big Data Increases Inequality and Threatens Democracy." Broadway Books, 2017.

5. Rosenzweig, Paul. "Cyber Warfare: How Conflicts in Cyberspace Are Challenging America and Changing the World." Praeger, 2012.

6. Solove, Daniel J. "Understanding Privacy." Harvard University Press, 2008.

7. Warford, Kevin E., et al. "Big Data Analytics: A Hands-On Approach." Morgan Kaufmann, 2020.

Encryption and Privacy Tools

In today's digital age, where data privacy and security are of utmost importance, encryption plays a critical role in ensuring the confidentiality and integrity of information. Encryption is the process of converting data into a form that is unreadable to unauthorized parties, known as ciphertext, using an encryption algorithm and a secret key. In this section, we will explore the principles of encryption and various privacy tools that are widely used to safeguard sensitive information.

Principles of Encryption

Encryption relies on the principles of cryptography, which is the science of secure communication. There are two primary types of encryption: symmetric encryption and asymmetric encryption.

Symmetric Encryption: Symmetric encryption, also known as secret-key encryption, uses a single key to both encrypt and decrypt data. This key must be kept secret and shared securely between the communicating parties. The encryption algorithm takes the plaintext and the secret key as input and produces the ciphertext. To decrypt the ciphertext and retrieve the original plaintext, the same secret key is used with the decryption algorithm.

The strength of symmetric encryption lies in the secrecy of the key. If an adversary gains access to the secret key, they can decrypt the ciphertext and obtain the original plaintext. Therefore, key management is a critical aspect of symmetric encryption systems.

Asymmetric Encryption: Asymmetric encryption, also known as public-key encryption, uses a pair of mathematically related keys: a public key and a private key. The public key is freely available to anyone, while the private key is kept secret by the owner.

The encryption algorithm uses the recipient's public key to encrypt the plaintext and produce the ciphertext. Only the recipient, who possesses the corresponding private key, can decrypt the ciphertext and obtain the original plaintext. This property eliminates the need for secure key distribution, as the public key can be openly shared.

Common Encryption Algorithms

Numerous encryption algorithms have been developed over the years, each with its own strengths and vulnerabilities. Let's explore some commonly used encryption algorithms and their applications:

- **Advanced Encryption Standard (AES):** AES is a symmetric encryption algorithm widely used to secure sensitive data. It supports key sizes of 128, 192, and 256 bits and is considered secure against all known practical attacks when used correctly.

- **Rivest-Shamir-Adleman (RSA):** RSA is an asymmetric encryption algorithm used for secure communication and digital signatures. It is based on the mathematical problem of factoring large composite numbers and relies on the difficulty of factorization for its security.

- **Elliptic Curve Cryptography (ECC):** ECC is an asymmetric encryption algorithm that uses the mathematics of elliptic curves to provide strong security with relatively short key lengths. This makes ECC particularly suitable for resource-constrained devices such as mobile phones.

- **Diffie-Hellman (DH):** DH is a key exchange protocol that allows two parties to establish a shared secret key securely over an insecure channel. It is widely used in secure communication protocols such as Secure Socket Layer/Transport Layer Security (SSL/TLS).

Privacy Tools

In addition to encryption algorithms, various privacy tools are available to protect personal data and mitigate privacy risks. Let's explore some commonly used privacy tools:

Virtual Private Networks (VPNs): A VPN encrypts internet traffic by routing it through a secure server before reaching its destination. This ensures the confidentiality and integrity of the data transmitted over public networks. VPNs are widely used to protect online privacy and secure remote connections.

Tor (The Onion Router): Tor is a network of volunteer-operated servers that allows users to browse the internet anonymously. It encrypts and routes network traffic through multiple relays, making it difficult to track the origin and destination of the data. Tor is often used by individuals who require anonymity, such as whistleblowers and journalists.

PGP/GPG: Pretty Good Privacy (PGP) and its open-source counterpart GnuPG (GPG) are encryption programs that provide privacy and authentication for data communication. They use asymmetric encryption to encrypt emails and files, ensuring that only the intended recipients can access the information.

Password Managers: Password managers are tools that securely store and manage passwords for various online accounts. They generate strong, random passwords and automatically fill them in when needed, reducing the risk of using weak or duplicated passwords.

Secure Messaging Apps: Secure messaging apps, such as Signal and WhatsApp, use end-to-end encryption to protect the privacy of conversations. End-to-end encryption ensures that only the sender and recipient can read the messages, preventing eavesdropping by third parties.

Real-World Example: Secure Messaging with Signal

Let's consider a real-world example of using the Signal app for secure messaging. Signal is an open-source messaging app that uses end-to-end encryption to ensure the privacy of conversations.

When Alice wants to send a secure message to Bob using Signal, the following process takes place:

1. Alice's Signal app generates a pair of asymmetric encryption keys: a public key and a private key. The private key is stored securely on Alice's device, and the public key is shared with others.

2. Alice's Signal app retrieves Bob's public key from the Signal server or from a key exchange between Alice and Bob.

3. Alice's Signal app encrypts the plaintext message using Bob's public key, generating the ciphertext.

4. The ciphertext is sent to Bob through the Signal server or directly if both parties are online.

5. Bob's Signal app, using Bob's private key stored on his device, decrypts the ciphertext and retrieves the original plaintext message.

By using Signal, Alice and Bob can be confident that their messages are secure and cannot be intercepted or read by unauthorized parties.

Caveats and Challenges

While encryption and privacy tools offer valuable protection, they are not without challenges and limitations. Here are some caveats to consider:

Key Management: Secure key management is crucial for maintaining the confidentiality of encrypted data. If a key is lost or compromised, the encrypted data may become inaccessible.

Backdoors and Vulnerabilities: Encryption algorithms and privacy tools are not immune to vulnerabilities or backdoors.

Flaws in software implementations or hidden vulnerabilities can compromise the security of the encryption.

Social Engineering: No encryption algorithm can protect against social engineering attacks, where an attacker convinces a user to disclose their secret key or password willingly. Users must exercise caution and follow best practices to avoid falling victim to such attacks.

Metadata and Traffic Analysis: While encryption protects the content of the communication, metadata such as the sender, recipient, and timestamps may still be visible. Metadata can be valuable for analyzing patterns and connections, potentially compromising privacy.

Emerging Technologies: As technology advances, new encryption algorithms and privacy tools will continue to emerge. Adapting to these technologies and ensuring compatibility between different systems can be a challenge.

Conclusion

Encryption and privacy tools play a crucial role in safeguarding sensitive information in the digital world. Whether it is protecting personal conversations or securing enterprise data, encryption ensures that data remains confidential and trustworthy. However, it is important to remain vigilant and stay informed about emerging technologies, vulnerabilities, and best practices to mitigate privacy risks effectively. With the rapid evolution of computing, encryption and privacy tools will continue to evolve, enabling individuals and organizations to navigate the digital landscape securely and confidently.

Bias in Algorithms

Fairness and Accountability in Computing

In today's increasingly digital world, computing technologies have become pervasive, affecting almost every aspect of our lives. From social media algorithms to hiring processes, computers and algorithms are being used to make decisions that have real-world consequences. However, there is growing concern about the fairness and accountability of these systems. As we rely more and more on automated decision-making, it is crucial to ensure that these systems are fair, transparent, and accountable. In this section, we will explore the concepts of fairness and accountability in computing and discuss the challenges and opportunities they present.

Understanding Fairness in Computing

Fairness, in the context of computing, refers to the impartial treatment of individuals by algorithms and automated systems. It is about ensuring that decisions made by machines do not result in unfair advantages or disadvantages for certain groups of people. However, defining and achieving fairness in computing is not a straightforward task. Different notions of fairness may conflict with each other, making it challenging to create algorithms that satisfy all of them simultaneously.

One common notion of fairness is **equality of opportunity**, which means that individuals should have an equal chance of being successful, regardless of their background or characteristics. For example, in the context of hiring, an algorithm that is fair with respect to equality of opportunity would consider candidates solely based on their qualifications, without any bias based on gender, race, or other protected characteristics.

Another important notion of fairness is **fairness through awareness**, which aims to address historical and societal biases that may exist in the data used by algorithms. If historical data contains biases, such as underrepresentation of certain groups, a fair algorithm should be aware of these biases and take them into account to ensure that the outcomes are fair for all groups. This means that the algorithm should strive to mitigate the impact of these biases and avoid perpetuating them.

Achieving fairness in computing is a complex and multidisciplinary task. It requires expertise from fields such as computer science, statistics, and social sciences. Researchers and practitioners are actively exploring different mathematical and algorithmic techniques to quantify and measure fairness, as well as tools and methodologies to test and assess the fairness of algorithms.

Challenges in Ensuring Fairness

Ensuring fairness in computing systems is not without its challenges. Here are some of the key challenges that need to be addressed:

1. **Problem of Bias:** One of the main challenges is dealing with bias in data that is used by algorithms. Biases can exist due to historical societal patterns or limitations in data collection methods. Addressing and mitigating bias requires careful analysis of the data used to train algorithms and the development of techniques to minimize the impact of bias on algorithmic outcomes.

2. **Trade-offs in Fairness Metrics:** As mentioned earlier, different notions of fairness may conflict with each other, making it difficult to optimize algorithms to satisfy all fairness criteria simultaneously. For example, ensuring equal error rates for different groups may lead to

disparities in other important metrics. Striking the right balance between different fairness metrics is a challenging problem that requires careful consideration.

3. **Interpretability and Transparency:** Fairness in algorithms is not just about the outcomes but also about how those outcomes are reached. Ensuring transparency and interpretability of algorithms is crucial to detect and address potential biases or discriminatory factors. However, many complex machine learning algorithms, such as deep neural networks, are often considered black boxes, making it challenging to decipher the decision-making process and understand the reasons behind a particular outcome.

4. **Adversarial Attacks:** Malicious actors may try to manipulate or exploit algorithmic systems to gain an unfair advantage. Adversarial attacks can target both the data used to train models and the decision-making process itself. Developing robust algorithms that are resistant to such attacks is an ongoing challenge in ensuring fairness and accountability.

Approaches to Ensuring Fairness

To address the challenges associated with fairness in computing, researchers and practitioners have proposed several approaches. Here are some of the commonly used techniques:

1. **Algorithmic Fairness:** Algorithmic fairness focuses on designing algorithms that are inherently fair and unbiased. This involves developing mathematical models and algorithms that explicitly incorporate fairness constraints and objectives. For example, fairness-aware machine learning algorithms aim to minimize disparate treatment

or impact across different groups while maintaining good predictive performance.

2. **Pre-processing and Post-processing:** Pre-processing and post-processing techniques modify the input data or the output of a model to ensure fairness. For example, pre-processing techniques may involve modifying the training data to remove biases or reweighing instances to ensure equal representation of different groups. Post-processing techniques modify the predictions of a trained model to ensure certain fairness criteria are met.

3. **Fairness in AI Governance:** Fairness in computing also requires attention at the societal and policy level. Establishing governance frameworks and policies that promote fairness and accountability is essential. This includes regulations that address algorithmic bias, data privacy, and transparency. It is crucial to involve diverse stakeholders, including experts from different disciplines and representatives from affected communities, in the development of such governance frameworks.

Case Study: Fairness in Credit Scoring

A real-world example that illustrates the importance of fairness in computing is credit scoring. Credit scoring algorithms play a crucial role in determining individuals' creditworthiness and eligibility for loans. However, if these algorithms are biased, they can result in unfair outcomes, disproportionately affecting certain groups of people.

Suppose a credit scoring algorithm relies on historical data from loan applicants to make predictions. If this historical data contains biases, such as underrepresentation of certain minority groups, the algorithm may inadvertently discriminate against those groups. For example, if the algorithm assigns higher credit scores to individuals from certain ethnic backgrounds, it can create a cycle of disadvantage, making it harder for individuals from disadvantaged groups to obtain credit and improve their financial situation.

To address this issue, fairness-aware credit scoring algorithms can be developed. These algorithms take into account the potential biases in the historical data and adjust the credit scoring process to ensure fairness. For example, they may use techniques like reweighing or equalizing odds to remove bias from the predictions and ensure equal treatment of individuals from different groups.

It is important to note that achieving fairness in credit scoring is not a one-size-fits-all approach. Different fairness criteria may be relevant in different contexts, and the choice of fairness metrics depends on societal values, legal requirements, and specific objectives. Examining the trade-offs and implications of different fairness approaches is key to ensuring a balanced and just credit scoring system.

Ethical Considerations

Ensuring fairness in computing is not just a technical challenge but also an ethical imperative. As algorithms increasingly make decisions that impact people's lives, it is crucial that these decisions are transparent, accountable, and aligned with societal values. Here are some key ethical considerations related to fairness in computing:

- **Transparency:** Algorithms should be transparent, and their decision-making process should be explainable. Individuals should have the right to know on what basis a decision affecting them has been made and have an opportunity to challenge it if necessary.

- **Accountability:** Organizations deploying algorithmic systems should be accountable for the decisions made by these systems. This includes mechanisms to monitor, evaluate, and address any biases or unfair outcomes resulting from the use of these systems.
- **Inclusivity:** Fairness requires inclusivity. Designing fair algorithms and systems requires diverse and inclusive teams that bring different perspectives and experiences to the table. This ensures a wider range of biases and risks are considered during the development process.
- **Continued Evaluation and Iteration:** Fairness is not a one-time achievement; it requires continuous evaluation and improvement. Organizations should regularly assess the impact of algorithms on different groups and be willing to iterate and refine their algorithms to mitigate any biases or disparities that arise.

By addressing these ethical considerations, we can foster a more equitable and just digital society that prioritizes fairness and accountability in computing.

Conclusion

Fairness and accountability in computing are crucial to ensure that the benefits of technology are distributed equally and that algorithms do not perpetuate or amplify existing biases and inequalities. Achieving fairness requires a multipronged approach, involving algorithmic techniques, governance frameworks, and ethical considerations. By striving for fairness and being accountable for the decisions made by our computing systems, we can create a more inclusive and just digital future.

In the next section, we will explore the concept of algorithmic bias and its implications for fairness in computing.

Exercises

1. Discuss some real-world examples where algorithmic systems have been found to be biased. What were the implications of these biases?

2. Research and compare different fairness metrics used in the evaluation of algorithms. What are the strengths and limitations of each metric?

3. Consider a decision-making process that relies on an algorithm, such as university admissions or employee screening. Identify potential biases that may arise in such a process, and propose fairness-aware techniques to mitigate those biases.

4. Explore the ethical considerations related to fairness in artificial intelligence. How can organizations develop ethical guidelines and processes to ensure fairness in their AI systems?

5. Investigate recent legal and regulatory developments addressing fairness in computing. How are different countries and jurisdictions approaching the issue of algorithmic fairness?

Resources

1. Hardt, M., Price, E., & Srebro, N. (2016). Equality of opportunity in supervised learning. In Advances in neural information processing systems (pp. 3315-3323).

2. Barocas, S., Hardt, M., & Narayanan, A. (2019). Fairness and machine learning. fairnessbook.org.

3. Buolamwini, J., & Gebru, T. (2018). Gender shades: Intersectional accuracy disparities in commercial gender classification. In Proceedings of the 1st Conference on Fairness, Accountability and Transparency (pp. 81-91).

4. Mittelstadt, B. D., Allo, P., Taddeo, M., Wachter, S., & Floridi, L. (2016). The ethics of algorithms: Mapping the debate. Big data & society, 3(2), 2053951716679679.

5. Zliobaite, I., & Kamiran, F. (2015). Handling conditional discrimination. arXiv preprint arXiv:1505.05723.

Further Reading

1. O'Neil, C. (2016). Weapons of Math Destruction: How Big Data Increases Inequality and Threatens Democracy. Crown.

2. Eubanks, V. (2018). Automating Inequality: How High-Tech Tools Profile, Police, and Punish the Poor. St. Martin's Press.

3. Noble, S. U. (2018). Algorithms of Oppression: How Search Engines Reinforce Racism. NYU Press.

4. Crawford, K. (2019). Automated Justice. Harv. L. Rev., 132, 1636.

5. Edwards, L., & Veale, M. (2017). Slave to the algorithm? Why a 'right to an explanation' is probably not the remedy you are looking for. Duke L. & Tech. Rev., 16, 18.

Algorithmic Bias in AI

Algorithmic bias refers to the phenomenon where AI-based systems produce unfair or discriminatory outcomes due to biases embedded in the algorithms or the data used to train them. While AI has the potential to revolutionize various domains, such as healthcare, finance, and criminal justice, the presence of bias in these systems can perpetuate discrimination and inequality. Understanding and addressing algorithmic bias is crucial to ensure fair and ethical use of AI technology.

Causes of Algorithmic Bias

Algorithmic bias can arise from several sources, including biased training data, biased algorithms, and biased decision-making processes.

One of the main causes of bias is biased training data. AI algorithms learn from historical data, and if the data used to train the algorithms contain systemic biases, the algorithms can perpetuate those biases in their predictions or recommendations. For example, if historical loan data used to train a credit scoring algorithm is biased against certain minority groups, the algorithm may unfairly deny loans to individuals from those groups.

Another cause of bias is biased algorithm design. Biased assumptions or preferences can be unintentionally (or intentionally) embedded into the design of an algorithm. For instance, an algorithm used in a job application screening process that favors candidates from certain educational backgrounds may perpetuate socioeconomic inequalities.

Biased decision-making processes can also contribute to algorithmic bias. Human biases in decision-making, such as confirmation bias or implicit biases, can influence the choices made during the development and deployment of AI systems, leading to biased outcomes.

Types of Algorithmic Bias

There are several types of algorithmic bias that can occur in AI systems:

- **Selection Bias:** This type of bias occurs when the training data used to train the algorithm does not accurately represent the population it is supposed to generalize to. For example, if a facial recognition system is primarily trained on images of light-skinned individuals, it may perform poorly when trying to recognize faces of people with darker skin tones.
- **Prejudice Bias:** Prejudice bias refers to biases that are explicitly encoded into the AI algorithm or the data used for training. These biases may reflect discriminatory attitudes or beliefs held by the creators of the AI system. For example, an AI-powered chatbot could be programmed to respond differently to users based on their gender, reinforcing gender stereotypes.
- **Measurement Bias:** Measurement bias occurs when the data used to evaluate or measure the performance of an AI system are biased or incomplete. For instance, if a predictive policing algorithm is evaluated based on biased arrest data, it may perpetuate the over-policing of certain communities.
- **Association Bias:** Association bias arises when an AI system makes unfair predictions or recommendations based on associations or correlations that exist in the training data but are not causally linked to the predicted outcome. For example, an AI system trained on recruitment data that is biased against women may unfairly associate gender with job performance, leading to biased hiring decisions.

Consequences of Algorithmic Bias

Algorithmic bias can have significant consequences in various areas. Here are a few examples:

- **Criminal Justice:** AI algorithms used in predicting the likelihood of reoffending or determining parole decisions can have biased outcomes. Biased predictions can lead to unfair and unequal treatment of individuals, especially those from marginalized communities.

- **Finance:** Credit scoring algorithms that exhibit bias can result in certain individuals or groups being denied loans or facing higher interest rates, contributing to financial disparities.

- **Healthcare:** Biased algorithms used in healthcare decisions, such as diagnosis or treatment recommendation systems, can result in unequal access to care and misdiagnoses, particularly among underrepresented groups.

- **Employment:** AI-based hiring systems that exhibit bias may perpetuate discriminatory practices and hinder diversity and inclusion efforts.

Addressing Algorithmic Bias

Addressing algorithmic bias requires a multi-faceted approach that involves various stakeholders, including developers, policymakers, and ethicists. Here are some strategies for mitigating algorithmic bias:

- **Transparency and Accountability:** Developers should strive for transparency by disclosing the factors that influence their algorithms' decisions. They should also establish mechanisms for external auditing and third-party evaluation of their systems to ensure accountability.

- **Diverse and Inclusive Data:** Training data should be diverse, representative, and inclusive of all relevant populations. The inclusion of underrepresented groups can help reduce bias and ensure fair outcomes.

- **Fairness Metrics and Evaluation:** Developers should define and measure fairness metrics to evaluate the performance of their algorithms and identify and address biases. Fairness metrics can help in detecting and mitigating disparate impact on protected groups.

- **Bias Detection and Debiasing Techniques:** Techniques such as bias detection algorithms and debiasing approaches, such as reweighing or post-processing, can be employed to identify and mitigate bias in AI systems.

- **Ethics Review Boards:** Organizations can establish ethics review boards or committees to ensure that the design and deployment of AI systems consider ethical implications and mitigate biases.

- **User Feedback and Redress:** Establishing mechanisms for users to provide feedback and seek recourse in case of biased outcomes can help identify and rectify algorithmic bias.

Case Study: Bias in Facial Recognition

One example of algorithmic bias is the biased performance of facial recognition systems. Research has shown that these systems exhibit higher error rates when attempting to recognize the faces of individuals with darker skin tones or women compared to lighter-skinned individuals and men. This bias primarily stems from the lack of diversity in the training datasets used to train these systems.

This bias can have serious implications, particularly in areas such as law enforcement, where facial recognition is used for identification and surveillance purposes. Misidentification of individuals can lead to wrongful arrests and further perpetuate systemic biases in the criminal justice system.

To mitigate bias in facial recognition systems, efforts should be made to ensure diverse representation in the training datasets. Furthermore, evaluating the performance of these systems on different demographic groups and actively working towards reducing disparities in performance is essential.

Conclusion

Algorithmic bias in AI is a significant concern that can impact various sectors of society, perpetuate discrimination, and exacerbate existing inequalities. Addressing and mitigating algorithmic bias requires a holistic approach involving developers, policymakers, researchers, and the broader public. Transparency, diverse training data, fairness evaluation, bias detection and debiasing techniques, and user feedback mechanisms are some of the strategies that can help ensure fair and ethical use of AI technology. As AI continues to evolve, it is essential to mitigate algorithmic bias to build a more equitable and just future.

Addressing Bias in Machine Learning Models

Bias in machine learning models refers to the systematic error or prejudice that can occur when the models are trained on biased data or when the algorithms themselves have inherent biases. These biases can perpetuate inequalities and discrimination, leading to unfair outcomes for certain groups of people.

Therefore, it is crucial to address bias in machine learning models to ensure fairness and equity.

Identifying Bias in Models

To address bias in machine learning models, the first step is to identify and understand the types of bias that can exist. Here are some common types of bias in machine learning:

- **Sampling Bias:** This bias occurs when the training data used to build the model does not represent the entire population accurately. For example, if a facial recognition system is trained primarily on data from lighter-skinned individuals, it may have reduced accuracy for darker-skinned individuals.

- **Labeling Bias:** Labeling bias refers to biases in the annotated or labeled data used to train the model. If the annotators have their own biases or if the data is labeled using biased criteria, the model can learn and perpetuate these biases.

- **Confirmation Bias:** Confirmation bias occurs when the models learn patterns that confirm existing stereotypes or preconceived notions. For example, if a hiring model is trained on historical hiring data that is biased against certain groups, it may continue to discriminate against those groups.

- **User Interaction Bias:** This bias arises from the users' interactions with the system. User feedback or behavior may introduce biases into the model. For instance, if a recommendation system predominantly recommends certain types of content to certain users, it can reinforce existing biases.

Addressing Bias in Training Data

To mitigate bias in machine learning models, it is essential to address biases present in the training data. Here are some strategies for doing so:

- **Data Collection:** When collecting data, it is crucial to ensure diversity and representativeness. Diverse datasets should include samples from various demographics, socioeconomic backgrounds, and geographic regions.
- **Data Preprocessing:** Preprocessing techniques can be applied to the training data to mitigate bias. For example, oversampling or undersampling techniques can be used to balance datasets in terms of representation.
- **Debiasing Techniques:** There are various debiasing techniques that can be applied, such as reweighting the training data to reduce the influence of biased samples, or modifying the loss function to penalize biased predictions.

Improving Model Fairness

In addition to addressing bias in training data, there are techniques for improving the fairness of machine learning models:

- **Fair Representation Learning:** Fair representation learning aims to learn representations of data that do not encode sensitive attributes. By removing sensitive information from the input data, models can focus on making fair decisions.
- **Model Regularization:** Regularization techniques, such as fairness constraints, can be applied during model training to ensure fairness. These constraints can enforce fairness by limiting the disparity in outcomes across different groups.

- **Post-processing:** After making predictions, post-processing techniques can be applied to adjust the outputs and ensure fairness. These techniques modify the model's outputs to reduce bias while still maintaining accuracy.

Evaluating and Monitoring Bias

To ensure ongoing fairness, it is important to evaluate and monitor bias in machine learning models. Here are some evaluation techniques:

- **Bias Metrics:** Various metrics can be used to quantify and measure bias in models. For example, disparate impact and equalized odds are commonly used to assess fairness in classification tasks.

- **Bias Testing:** Dedicated bias testing can be performed by comparing the performance of the model across different demographic groups. This testing helps identify disparate treatment or unfavorable outcomes for specific groups.

- **Real-world Monitoring:** Responsible implementation of machine learning models requires continuous monitoring in real-world scenarios to detect and address any disparities or biases that may arise.

Ethical Considerations

Addressing bias in machine learning models goes beyond technical solutions; it requires careful considerations of ethical aspects. Here are some ethical considerations in addressing bias:

- **Transparency:** The decision-making process of models should be transparent and explainable to ensure accountability and trust. This includes explaining how bias is addressed and how fairness is ensured.

- **User Feedback:** Incorporating user feedback is critical to capturing biases or issues that may not have been identified during development. Users should have ways to report and provide input on model outcomes.

- **Diverse Development Teams:** Building diverse teams that include individuals from different backgrounds and perspectives can help identify and mitigate bias during model development.

Addressing bias in machine learning models is an ongoing challenge, as biases can evolve or be introduced due to changing societal dynamics. It requires a multi-disciplinary approach, considering technical, ethical, and societal aspects to ensure fairness and equity in the application of machine learning.

Case Study: Bias in Facial Recognition Systems

One well-known example where bias in machine learning models has garnered attention is in facial recognition systems. These systems have been found to have higher error rates for women and people of color, primarily due to biases in the training data. This bias can lead to unfair treatment, such as misidentification or increased surveillance for certain groups.

To address this bias, researchers and developers have been working on various techniques. For example, diverse and representative datasets are being used to train facial recognition models, which include a balanced representation of different genders, ethnicities, and age groups. Additionally, researchers are exploring approaches to reduce the impact of demographic factors on the performance of facial recognition systems. By improving data collection practices and algorithmic design, the aim is to build more accurate and fair facial recognition systems.

However, it is important to note that while progress is being made, bias in facial recognition systems and other machine learning models is a complex and ongoing challenge. Continued research, collaboration, and ethical considerations are necessary to ensure that these technologies are fair and beneficial for all individuals and communities.

Further Reading

For further exploration of bias in machine learning models, the following resources provide valuable insights and discussions:

- Barocas, S., & Selbst, A. D. (2016). *Big data's disparate impact.* California Law Review, 104(3), 671-732.

- Buolamwini, J., & Gebru, T. (2018). *Gender shades: Intersectional accuracy disparities in commercial gender classification.* Proceedings of the 1st Conference on Fairness, Accountability, and Transparency, 77-91.

- Mitchell, M., Gebru, T., & Dumoulin, V. (2019). *Towards a definition of fairness in machine learning.* Proceedings of the 2018 FAT/ML conference.

- Narayanan, A., & Reddy, N. (2017). *How to make a decision: Models, biases, and algorithms.* Proceedings of AI Now Symposium.

These resources provide in-depth analysis, case studies, and ethical perspectives on bias in machine learning models, guiding researchers, practitioners, and policymakers in addressing bias and ensuring fairness in the field of machine learning.

Cybersecurity and Digital Threats

Evolution of Cybersecurity

In today's interconnected digital world, cybersecurity has become a critical aspect of our lives. With the increasing reliance on technology and the growing threat of cyber attacks, understanding the evolution of cybersecurity is essential for protecting ourselves and our digital assets. In this section, we will explore the key milestones and developments in the field of cybersecurity, from its early beginnings to the challenges we face today.

Early Security Measures

The need for security in computing systems arose soon after their inception. In the early days, computer security focused primarily on physical controls, such as locked rooms and limited access to computer facilities. However, as technology advanced, so did the sophistication of cyber threats.

In the 1970s, the introduction of time-sharing systems allowed multiple users to access a single computer simultaneously. This brought new challenges in ensuring the privacy and integrity of users' data. To address these challenges, encryption techniques, such as the Data Encryption Standard (DES), were developed to protect sensitive information from unauthorized access.

The Rise of Hacking

With the advent of the internet in the 1990s, a new breed of cyber threats emerged. Hackers, individuals with advanced computer skills, began exploiting vulnerabilities in computer networks and systems. This marked a significant shift in the history of cybersecurity, as it brought the concept of proactive defense to the forefront.

As hackers became more sophisticated, businesses and organizations started investing in firewalls and intrusion detection systems to detect and prevent unauthorized access to their networks. However, these measures proved to be inadequate in the face of rapidly evolving cyber threats.

The Need for Cybersecurity Frameworks

The early 2000s saw a growing recognition of the need for comprehensive cybersecurity frameworks to protect critical infrastructure and sensitive data. Governments and international organizations began developing standards and guidelines to establish best practices for cybersecurity.

One such framework is the National Institute of Standards and Technology's (NIST) Cybersecurity Framework. It provides organizations with a set of voluntary guidelines and best practices to manage and reduce cybersecurity risks. The framework consists of five core functions: Identify, Protect, Detect, Respond, and Recover, which serve as a roadmap for organizations to develop and maintain their cybersecurity posture.

Emerging Threats: Malware and Ransomware

As technology continues to advance, so do the threats to cybersecurity. Malicious software, or malware, has become a common tool used by cybercriminals to gain unauthorized access to computer systems and networks. Malware can take various forms, such as viruses, worms, Trojans, and spyware. These malicious programs can cause significant damage by stealing sensitive information, disrupting computer operations, or even rendering systems inoperable.

In recent years, a particularly alarming form of malware, known as ransomware, has gained prominence. Ransomware encrypts a victim's files or locks them out of their system entirely, demanding a ransom in exchange for restoring access. This type of attack has targeted individuals, businesses, and even government agencies, causing financial losses and significant disruptions.

Cybersecurity and Artificial Intelligence

With the increasing complexity and scale of cyber threats, the field of cybersecurity is turning to artificial intelligence (AI) for defense. AI-powered cybersecurity systems can analyze vast amounts of data, detect patterns, and recognize anomalies that may indicate a cyber attack. This proactive approach helps organizations identify and mitigate threats more efficiently.

However, while AI offers significant benefits in cybersecurity, it also presents new challenges. Adversarial AI, where malicious actors exploit vulnerabilities in AI systems, is a growing concern. Hackers can utilize AI algorithms to launch sophisticated attacks that evade traditional defenses. As a result, the ongoing development of AI-powered cybersecurity systems must keep pace with evolving threats.

Security in the Internet of Things (IoT)

The Internet of Things (IoT) brings connectivity to everyday objects, providing convenience and efficiency. However, the proliferation of IoT devices also raises security concerns. Many IoT devices lack robust security measures, making them vulnerable to cyber attacks.

Unauthorized access to IoT devices can have serious consequences. For example, a compromised IoT device can become a gateway for hackers to gain access to a home network, compromising personal data or launching attacks on other connected devices. To address this issue, manufacturers and organizations are working to improve IoT security standards and implement stronger authentication and encryption mechanisms.

Building a Security-minded Culture

Ultimately, ensuring effective cybersecurity requires more than just technological measures. It requires a shift in mindset and a security-minded culture that fosters awareness and best practices among individuals and organizations. This involves ongoing education and training, regular security audits, and the adoption of robust security policies and procedures.

Organizations must also establish incident response plans to effectively handle and recover from cyber attacks. These plans outline the steps to be taken in the event of a security breach, including containment, investigation, and restoration of affected systems.

Conclusion

The evolution of cybersecurity mirrors the advancements in technology and the ever-changing threat landscape. From the early security measures to the rise of hacking and the emergence of sophisticated threats, the need for robust cybersecurity has never been greater.

As we continue to rely on technology in our daily lives, it is essential to understand the evolving nature of cyber threats and stay vigilant against them. By adopting a proactive and comprehensive approach to cybersecurity, we can protect our digital assets and maintain the integrity of our interconnected world.

Cyber Attacks and Defense Strategies

Cyber attacks refer to malicious attempts by individuals or groups to compromise computer systems, networks, and data, with the intentions of unauthorized access, theft, disruption, or destruction. As technology continues to advance, the sophistication and frequency of cyber attacks have increased, making it crucial for organizations and individuals to understand and implement effective defense strategies. In this section, we will explore various types of cyber attacks and discuss strategies to defend against them.

Types of Cyber Attacks

1. **Malware Attacks:** Malware, short for malicious software, encompasses a range of harmful programs designed to exploit vulnerabilities in computer systems. Some common types of malware attacks include:

- *Viruses*: Infects host files or programs, replicates itself, and spreads to other systems when the infected files or programs are shared.
- *Worms*: Self-replicating programs that spread across networks, exploiting security weaknesses and causing damage to systems.
- *Trojans*: Disguised as legitimate software, Trojans trick users into executing them, allowing attackers to gain unauthorized access or control over the infected system.
- *Ransomware*: Encrypts files or locks users out of their systems until a ransom is paid to the attackers.

2. **Phishing Attacks:** Phishing attacks involve sending fraudulent emails or messages that appear to be from a

trustworthy source, aiming to deceive recipients into sharing sensitive information like passwords or financial details. Attackers often use social engineering techniques to manipulate users into taking actions that benefit the attacker.

3. **DDoS Attacks:** Distributed Denial of Service (DDoS) attacks involve overwhelming a target system with a massive amount of traffic or requests, rendering it inaccessible to legitimate users. These attacks typically use a botnet, a network of compromised computers, to flood the target with traffic.

4. **Man-in-the-Middle (MitM) Attacks:** In MitM attacks, attackers intercept and alter communications between two parties without their knowledge. By exploiting vulnerabilities in network protocols or through physical access to network infrastructure, attackers can eavesdrop, modify, or inject malicious content into the communication.

5. **SQL Injection Attacks:** SQL injection attacks target web applications that interact with a database. By inserting malicious SQL queries into user input fields, attackers can manipulate the application's database and gain unauthorized access, retrieve sensitive information, or modify data.

Defense Strategies

1. **Strong Authentication and Access Control:** Implementing strong authentication mechanisms, such as multi-factor authentication (MFA), helps ensure that only authorized users can access systems and resources. Additionally, using strong access control policies, such as the principle of least privilege, restricts users' access to only what is necessary for their roles, minimizing the potential impact of a compromised account.

2. **Regular Security Updates:** Keeping software, operating systems, and applications up to date is crucial to address known vulnerabilities. Regularly applying security patches and updates

ensures that systems are protected against known exploits, reducing the risk of successful attacks.

3. **Network Segmentation:** Dividing a network into smaller segments or subnetworks enhances security by limiting the impact of a compromised system or unauthorized access. This practice prevents attackers from easily moving laterally through the network and helps contain the damage in case of a breach.

4. **Encryption and Secure Communication:** Implementing encryption mechanisms, such as Transport Layer Security (TLS) protocols, ensures that data transmitted over networks is protected from unauthorized access. Encryption secures data at rest as well, by using strong encryption algorithms and proper key management practices.

5. **Employee Training and Awareness:** Educating employees about best practices for cybersecurity, including recognizing phishing emails, avoiding suspicious downloads, and using strong passwords, is essential to prevent successful attacks. Regular training and awareness programs help create a security-conscious workforce that can identify and report potential threats.

6. **Incident Response Planning:** Developing an incident response plan enables organizations to respond effectively to cyber attacks. This plan should include procedures for identifying, containing, eradicating, and recovering from a security incident, as well as guidelines for communication and coordination with relevant stakeholders.

7. **Regular Backup and Recovery:** Keeping regular backups of critical data helps organizations recover from ransomware attacks or other data loss incidents. It is essential to ensure that backups are stored securely and are tested regularly to verify their integrity and effectiveness.

Real-World Example

A notable cyber attack that demonstrates the importance of defense strategies is the 2017 WannaCry ransomware attack. This attack targeted thousands of organizations, encrypting their files and demanding a ransom for their release. The attack exploited a vulnerability in the Windows operating system, known as EternalBlue, which had been patched by Microsoft two months prior. Organizations that had not applied the security update fell victim to the attack.

This incident highlights the significance of regular security updates and patch management. Organizations that promptly applied the patch were protected from the attack. Additionally, organizations with robust backup strategies were able to recover their data without paying the ransom. The WannaCry attack serves as a reminder of the need for proactive defense measures to prevent, detect, and mitigate cyber threats.

Additional Resources

In addition to the strategies mentioned above, there are numerous other defense measures organizations can implement to protect against cyber attacks. They can include implementing intrusion detection and prevention systems, deploying next-generation firewalls, conducting regular vulnerability assessments and penetration testing, and establishing security incident and event management systems.

For further study and practical implementation of defense strategies, the following resources are recommended:

- "Cybersecurity for Beginners" by Raef Meeuwisse
- "The Web Application Hacker's Handbook" by Dafydd Stuttard and Marcus Pinto

- "Network Security Essentials: Applications and Standards" by William Stallings
- Online cybersecurity courses and certifications offered by institutions like Cybrary, SANS Institute, and Coursera.

Remember, cybersecurity is an ever-evolving field, and staying updated with the latest threats, vulnerabilities, and defensive techniques is crucial for maintaining a resilient defense against cyber attacks.

Exercises

1. **True or False:** A virus is a type of malware that can spread from one computer to another by attaching itself to files or programs.

2. **Short Answer:** What is the primary goal of a phishing attack?

3. **Short Answer:** Explain how a DDoS attack can render a target system inaccessible.

4. **Short Answer:** What is the purpose of network segmentation in cybersecurity?

5. **Discussion:** Research and discuss a recent cyber attack that occurred in your country or region. What were the methods used in the attack, and what defenses could have been employed to prevent or mitigate it?

Tricks and Caveats

- Beware of social engineering techniques used in phishing attacks. Always verify the authenticity of emails or messages before sharing sensitive information.

- Regularly update all software, including operating systems, applications, and plugins, to protect against known vulnerabilities.

- Develop and test an incident response plan to ensure a swift and effective response to a cyber attack.

- When implementing encryption, ensure the use of strong encryption algorithms and proper key management practices.

Remember, cybersecurity is a shared responsibility. Stay vigilant, stay informed, and adopt best practices to safeguard against cyber threats.

Conclusion

In this section, we explored the various types of cyber attacks that pose a threat to computer systems and networks. We discussed defense strategies such as strong authentication and access control, regular security updates, network segmentation, encryption, employee training and awareness, incident response planning, and regular backup and recovery.

To reinforce your understanding, we provided a real-world example of a significant cyber attack and highlighted the importance of defense measures. We also offered additional resources for further study and recommended exercises to test your knowledge.

As technology continues to evolve, so do the techniques employed by cyber attackers. Therefore, it is essential to remain vigilant, stay informed about the latest threats, and consistently update your defense strategies. By implementing effective defense measures and fostering a cybersecurity-conscious environment, individuals and organizations can reduce the risk of successful cyber attacks and protect their valuable assets. The constantly evolving landscape of cybersecurity necessitates ongoing adaptation and proactive measures to ensure the security and integrity of computer systems and networks.

"The History of Computing" has covered a wide range of topics, from pre-computing devices to the future prospects of quantum computing and human augmentation. We hope this book has provided you with a comprehensive understanding of the history, advancements, and impact of computing. May it inspire you to explore further and contribute to the exciting and ever-evolving field of computing.

Future Prospects

Quantum Computing Applications

Quantum Cryptography

Quantum cryptography is a field that explores the use of quantum mechanics to provide secure communication between two parties. The fundamental principles of quantum mechanics, such as the principles of superposition and entanglement, form the basis for the security of quantum cryptography protocols. In this section, we will discuss the principles of quantum cryptography, its applications, and its advantages over classical cryptography.

Principles of Quantum Cryptography

The main idea behind quantum cryptography is the use of quantum properties to securely transmit information. Two key principles of quantum mechanics are used in quantum cryptography: superposition and entanglement.

Superposition: According to the principle of superposition, a quantum system can exist in multiple states simultaneously. In the context of quantum cryptography, this means that a quantum bit (qubit) can be in a superposition of both 0 and 1 states at the same time.

Entanglement: Entanglement is a phenomenon in which two or more quantum particles become correlated in such a way that the state of one particle cannot be described independently of the others. In quantum cryptography, entanglement is used to establish a shared secret key between the sender and the receiver.

Quantum Key Distribution (QKD)

One of the most important applications of quantum cryptography is quantum key distribution (QKD). QKD allows two parties, often referred to as Alice and Bob, to securely exchange a secret key over an insecure communication channel. The security of QKD is based on the laws of quantum mechanics, making it resistant to attacks from eavesdroppers.

The most widely used QKD protocol is the BB84 protocol, developed by Charles Bennett and Gilles Brassard in 1984. The BB84 protocol involves the following steps:

1. **Key Generation:** Alice prepares a sequence of qubits in a random combination of basis states. Each qubit represents a bit of the secret key. She then sends the qubits to Bob.

2. **Measurement:** Bob randomly chooses a basis (e.g., the rectilinear basis or the diagonal basis) to measure each qubit he receives from Alice.

3. **Public Discussion:** Alice and Bob publicly share the basis they used for each qubit without revealing the actual measurement results.

4. **Key Distillation:** Alice and Bob compare subsets of their measurement results to detect errors caused by noise or eavesdropping. They discard the qubits that resulted in measurement errors.

5. **Reconciliation and Privacy Amplification:** Alice and Bob perform error correction and privacy amplification protocols to distill a final, secure key from the remaining qubits.

At the end of the protocol, Alice and Bob have a shared secret key that can be used for secure communication using symmetric encryption algorithms.

Advantages of Quantum Cryptography

Quantum cryptography offers several advantages over classical cryptography:

Security: The security of a quantum cryptography protocol is based on the laws of physics rather than computational complexity. It is provably secure against eavesdropping attacks, even if the attacker has unlimited computing power.

Detection of Eavesdropping: Quantum cryptography protocols have built-in mechanisms to detect eavesdropping attempts. Any attempt to intercept the qubits will introduce errors in the measurement results, alerting Alice and Bob to the presence of an eavesdropper.

Unconditional Security of the Key: The security of the secret key distribution in quantum cryptography is not based on assumptions about the computational power of an attacker. It provides unconditional security, meaning that no amount of computational power can break the security of the key.

Current Challenges and Limitations

While quantum cryptography offers many advantages, there are still challenges and limitations that need to be addressed:

Practical Implementation: The practical implementation of quantum cryptography protocols is still challenging. Current implementations require specialized equipment and operate at low data rates, making them impractical for many real-world applications.

Key Distribution Distance: The distance over which a secret key can be securely distributed using quantum cryptography is limited. The performance of quantum key distribution systems degrades with increasing distance due to losses in the communication channel.

Secure Key Storage: Once a secret key is generated using QKD, it needs to be securely stored until it is used for encryption. Ensuring the secure storage of the key is an ongoing challenge in quantum cryptography.

Quantum Cryptography in Practice

Despite the current challenges, quantum cryptography is being actively researched and developed for practical applications. Some of the areas where quantum cryptography is being explored include:

Secure Communication Networks: Quantum cryptography can be used to enhance the security of communication networks, such as banking systems, government communication, and military networks. QKD can provide a higher level of security for transmitting sensitive information.

Quantum Key Management: Quantum cryptography can also be used for secure key management in conventional encryption systems. QKD can be used to distribute the initial secret key, which is then used to encrypt and decrypt information using classical encryption algorithms.

Post-Quantum Cryptography: Quantum computers have the potential to break many of the current cryptographic algorithms used for secure communication. This has led to the development of post-quantum cryptography, which aims to create encryption algorithms that are resistant to attacks by both classical and quantum computers.

Summary

Quantum cryptography leverages the principles of quantum mechanics to provide secure communication between two parties. Quantum key distribution protocols, such as the BB84 protocol, allow for the secure exchange of secret keys over insecure communication channels. Quantum cryptography offers advantages such as unconditional security and the detection of eavesdropping attempts. However, practical implementation, limited key distribution distance, and secure key storage are current challenges in the field. Despite these challenges, quantum cryptography has promising applications in secure communication networks, quantum key management, and post-quantum cryptography. The ongoing evolution of quantum cryptography will continue to shape the future of secure communication.

Optimization Problems and Quantum Computing

In this section, we will explore the relationship between optimization problems and quantum computing. Optimization is a fundamental concept in computer science and mathematics, with applications in various fields such as finance, logistics, and engineering. Traditional optimization algorithms often face challenges when dealing with large-scale problems or complex constraints. Quantum computing, on the other hand, holds the potential to address these challenges by leveraging its unique properties such as superposition and entanglement.

Introduction to Optimization Problems

Before delving into the connection between optimization problems and quantum computing, let's start by understanding the basics of optimization problems.

An optimization problem involves finding the best possible solution among a set of available alternatives. This can be achieved by minimizing or maximizing an objective function, subject to a set of constraints. The objective function represents the quantity that needs to be optimized, while the constraints represent the limitations or conditions that must be satisfied.

There are two primary types of optimization problems:

1. *Continuous optimization problems,* where the variables can take any real value within a specified range. Examples include minimizing the cost of production given certain constraints or maximizing the profit from an investment portfolio.

2. *Combinatorial optimization problems,* where the variables are discrete and can only take specific values from a finite set. Examples include finding the shortest path in a graph or determining an optimal assignment of tasks to workers.

Solving optimization problems typically requires searching through a large solution space to find the optimal solution. Traditional algorithms, such as gradient-based methods or branch-and-bound algorithms, are often used to solve optimization problems efficiently. However, they can become computationally expensive or inefficient for certain types of complex optimization problems.

Quantum Computing and Optimization

Quantum computing, with its ability to perform calculations in parallel and exploit quantum phenomena, offers a promising approach to tackling optimization problems. By utilizing the principles of superposition and entanglement, a quantum computer can explore multiple potential solutions simultaneously, potentially leading to more efficient algorithms for optimization.

One of the most well-known quantum algorithms for optimization is the Quantum Approximate Optimization Algorithm (QAOA). QAOA is a variation of the Quantum Adiabatic Optimization Algorithm (QAOA), which was inspired by the adiabatic theorem in quantum mechanics. The goal of the QAOA is to find the optimal solution to an optimization problem by evolving a quantum system from an initial state to a final state, with the final state encoding the desired solution.

The QAOA algorithm has been successfully applied to various combinatorial optimization problems, including the Max-Cut problem and the Traveling Salesman Problem (TSP). While the solutions obtained by QAOA are not guaranteed to be optimal, they often provide good approximations to the optimal solution in a more efficient manner than classical algorithms.

Example: Traveling Salesman Problem (TSP)

To illustrate the application of quantum computing in solving optimization problems, let's consider the Traveling Salesman Problem (TSP). The TSP is a well-known combinatorial optimization problem that seeks to find the shortest possible route, also known as the Hamiltonian cycle, that visits a given set of cities and returns to the starting city.

Classically, finding the optimal solution for the TSP becomes increasingly difficult as the number of cities increases. The number of possible routes grows exponentially with the number of cities, making it computationally infeasible to solve the TSP for large instances.

Quantum algorithms, such as QAOA, offer a potential solution to efficiently solve the TSP. By encoding the TSP instance into a quantum system and leveraging quantum operations, a quantum computer can explore many possible routes simultaneously and converge to a good approximation of the optimal solution.

It's worth mentioning that while quantum algorithms show promise in solving optimization problems, their practical implementation faces challenges such as the need for error correction, the limited number of qubits in current quantum computers, and the existence of decoherence effects. Overcoming these challenges is crucial for the widespread adoption of quantum computing in optimization and other domains.

Resources and Further Reading

If you're interested in learning more about optimization problems and quantum computing, here are some recommended resources:

- *Quantum Computing for Optimization* by Andras Gilyen, et al.
- *Quantum Optimization and Applications* edited by Xin-She Yang, et al.
- *Quantum Computing: An Applied Approach* by Jack D. Hidary.
- *Quantum Computing Since Democritus* by Scott Aaronson.

Additionally, you may consider exploring research papers and articles on quantum algorithms for optimization, such as "A Quantum Approximate Optimization Algorithm" by Edward Farhi, et al., and "Quantum Computing in the NISQ era and beyond" by John Preskill.

Conclusion

In this section, we have explored the connection between optimization problems and quantum computing. Optimization problems play a crucial role in various fields, and quantum computing offers a promising approach to improving the efficiency of solving such problems. We have discussed the basics of optimization problems, the potential of quantum computing for solving optimization problems, and provided an example of applying quantum computing to the Traveling Salesman Problem. While quantum algorithms for optimization have shown promise, challenges remain in implementing them on current quantum hardware. Continued research and development in quantum computing will help unlock its full potential in solving complex optimization problems and pave the way for future advancements in the field.

AI and Human Augmentation

Brain-Computer Interfaces

Brain-Computer Interfaces (BCIs) are innovative technologies that enable direct communication and interaction between the human brain and computers or external devices. BCIs have the potential to revolutionize the way we interact with technology and have a significant impact on various fields, including healthcare, gaming, and assistive technology. In this section, we will explore the principles behind BCIs, their applications, challenges, and future prospects.

Principles of Brain-Computer Interfaces

BCIs work by detecting and interpreting brain signals to translate them into actionable commands. These signals are typically captured using a variety of sensors, such as electroencephalography (EEG), functional magnetic resonance imaging (fMRI), or invasive intracranial electrodes. EEG is the most common non-invasive method used in BCIs due to its affordability and portability.

The core principle of BCIs is to analyze the recorded brain signals and decode the user's intention or mental state. This involves identifying patterns or neural correlates associated with specific tasks, such as imagining the movement of a limb or focusing attention on a particular object. Machine learning algorithms, such as support vector machines or artificial neural networks, are often employed to analyze the brain signals and classify the user's intent accurately.

Applications of Brain-Computer Interfaces

BCIs have diverse applications across several domains:

Assistive Technology: BCIs can provide a means of communication and control for individuals with severe motor disabilities, such as locked-in syndrome or spinal cord injuries. By using BCIs, these individuals can operate assistive devices like robotic arms or computer interfaces just by utilizing their brain signals.

Healthcare and Rehabilitation: BCIs offer new possibilities for diagnosing and treating neurological disorders. They can be used to monitor brain activity during rehabilitation processes and provide feedback to healthcare professionals. BCIs also hold promise for restoring movement or sensory functions in patients with paralysis or sensory impairments through brain-controlled prosthetic devices.

Gaming and Entertainment: BCIs have found applications in the gaming industry, enabling users to control virtual characters or interact with virtual environments using their thoughts. This immersive and intuitive gameplay experience opens up new avenues for virtual reality (VR) and augmented reality (AR) applications.

Challenges and Limitations

Despite their potential, BCIs face several challenges that need to be addressed for wider adoption:

Signal Quality and Noise: Brain signals recorded using non-invasive methods like EEG are weak and easily contaminated by various sources of noise. Ensuring high-quality signal acquisition is crucial for accurate and reliable BCI performance.

User Training and Adaptation: BCIs require users to undergo extensive training to learn how to control their brain signals voluntarily. The learning process can be time-consuming and frustrating for some individuals, limiting the accessibility and usability of BCIs.

Interpretation Complexity: Decoding brain signals into meaningful actions or commands is a complex task. Developing sophisticated algorithms and models that can accurately interpret the user's intent from recorded brain signals remains a significant challenge.

Ethical Considerations

The development and application of BCIs raise important ethical considerations that need to be carefully addressed:

Privacy and Security: BCIs handle highly sensitive information related to a person's mental state and intentions. Ensuring the privacy and security of this information is critical to prevent unauthorized access or misuse.

Informed Consent: BCIs involve direct access to a person's brain signals and require informed consent to ensure that individuals fully understand the potential risks, benefits, and limitations of using the technology.

Stigmatization and Discrimination: The use of BCIs may lead to stigmatization or discrimination against individuals with neural impairments or modifications. It is essential to promote inclusivity and avoid societal biases when integrating BCIs into various contexts.

Future Prospects

The future of BCIs holds immense potential for further advancements and applications:

Improved Signal Acquisition: Ongoing research aims to develop better sensors and signal processing techniques to improve the quality of recorded brain signals, enhancing the accuracy and robustness of BCIs.

Enhanced Training Paradigms: Efforts are being made to develop more effective and efficient user training methods to reduce the learning curve associated with BCIs. This includes gamified training programs and adaptive algorithms that personalize the training process.

Closed-Loop BCIs: Closed-loop BCIs aim to establish bidirectional communication between the brain and the external device, allowing the system to adapt and provide real-time feedback, which can further enhance the user experience and performance.

Conclusion

BCIs have the potential to transform the way we interact with technology and improve the lives of individuals with neurological disorders or disabilities. By bridging the gap between the human brain and computers, BCIs open up exciting possibilities for healthcare, assistive technology, gaming, and beyond. However, significant challenges, including signal quality, user training, and ethical considerations, must be overcome to fully realize the potential of BCIs. Ongoing advancements in technology and research continue to push the boundaries of what is possible, driving us closer to a future where BCIs are seamlessly integrated into our daily lives.

Augmented Reality and Virtual Reality

Augmented Reality (AR) and Virtual Reality (VR) are two rapidly advancing technologies that are transforming the way we experience and interact with the digital world. Both AR and VR create immersive environments, but they differ in their approach and level of immersion.

Introduction to Augmented Reality and Virtual Reality

Augmented Reality overlays digital information onto the real world, enhancing our perception and interaction with our surroundings. AR technologies use various input devices, such as wearable glasses or smartphones, to blend computer-generated information with the real world in real time. The user can still see and interact with the physical environment while additional virtual information is seamlessly integrated.

Virtual Reality, on the other hand, creates a fully immersive digital environment that completely replaces the real world. Users wear a head-mounted display (HMD) that covers their eyes and ears, shutting out the physical world and transporting them to a simulated environment. VR technologies often incorporate other sensory experiences, such as haptic feedback and spatial audio, to enhance the sense of presence and immersion.

Principles of Augmented Reality

AR systems rely on several key principles to seamlessly integrate virtual information with the real world:

- **Tracking:** AR devices use sensors and cameras to track the user's movements and register them in virtual space. This allows virtual objects to move and interact with the real world in a realistic manner.

- **Registration:** AR systems need to accurately align virtual content with the physical environment. This involves mapping the real-world coordinates to virtual coordinates and ensuring that virtual objects appear in the correct position and orientation.

- **Overlay:** AR overlays virtual information onto the user's view of the real world. This can involve placing 3D objects, displaying text or graphics, or adding contextual information to real-world objects.

- **Interaction:** AR devices enable users to interact with virtual objects or information overlaid on the real world. This can be done through gestures, voice commands, or other input methods, allowing users to manipulate and engage with the augmented content.

Applications of Augmented Reality

Augmented Reality has a wide range of applications across various industries:

- **Gaming and Entertainment:** AR has revolutionized the gaming industry by allowing players to interact with virtual characters and objects in the real world. It has also been used to enhance live events, such as concerts and sports games, by overlaying additional information and graphics for spectators.

- **Education and Training:** AR has great potential in education and training, offering immersive and interactive experiences. It can provide virtual tours of historical sites, virtual dissections in biology classes, or simulations for training in various professional fields.

- **Architecture and Design:** AR enables architects and designers to visualize their projects in the real world before construction begins. It allows them to overlay 3D models onto physical spaces, enabling better spatial understanding and design iteration.

- **Healthcare:** AR is being used in healthcare for medical training, surgical planning, and visualization of patient data. Surgeons can use AR to overlay CT scans or X-ray images onto a patient's body during surgery, improving precision and reducing risks.

- **Retail and E-Commerce:** AR is transforming the retail experience by allowing virtual try-ons of clothing and accessories, visualizing furniture and home decor in real spaces, and providing additional product information through AR tags and labels.

Principles of Virtual Reality

Virtual Reality relies on the following principles to create a high level of immersion and presence:

- **Immersion:** VR aims to create a sense of presence, making users feel fully immersed in the virtual environment. This involves providing a wide field of view, high-quality visuals, and realistic audio to stimulate the user's senses.

- **Interaction:** VR systems enable users to interact with the virtual environment through various input devices, such as hand controllers or motion trackers. This allows users to manipulate objects, navigate the virtual space, and engage with the virtual world.

- **Spatial Audio:** VR often incorporates spatial audio technologies to create a realistic sound environment. Sounds are positioned in 3D space, providing directional audio cues that enhance the sense of immersion and presence.
- **Haptic Feedback:** VR devices can provide haptic feedback, allowing users to feel physical sensations in the virtual world. This can range from simple vibrations to more advanced haptic systems that provide a sense of touch and texture.

Applications of Virtual Reality

Virtual Reality has numerous applications across different industries:

- **Gaming and Simulation:** VR has revolutionized the gaming industry, offering players an immersive and interactive gaming experience. It has also been used for virtual simulations, such as flight simulators, driving training, and medical simulations.
- **Education and Training:** VR can provide immersive educational experiences, allowing students to explore historical events, visit famous landmarks, or dive into scientific concepts. It is also used for training purposes, such as virtual on-the-job training or virtual simulations for high-risk environments.
- **Design and Visualization:** VR enables architects, engineers, and designers to visualize their creations in 3D and experience them at a human scale. It allows users to walk through virtual buildings, explore virtual landscapes, and make design decisions based on realistic representations.

- **Healthcare and Therapy:** VR is used in healthcare for pain management, exposure therapy, and rehabilitation. It can simulate real-life scenarios to help patients overcome phobias or provide a distraction from pain during medical procedures.

- **Virtual Tourism:** VR can transport users to faraway places, offering virtual tours and experiences of tourist destinations. It allows users to explore museums, historical sites, and even underwater environments without leaving their homes.

Challenges and Future Directions

While AR and VR have made significant advancements, there are still challenges to overcome:

- **Hardware Limitations:** AR and VR systems often require powerful hardware to deliver immersive experiences. Improvements in display resolution, field of view, and ergonomics are needed to enhance user comfort and reduce the barrier to entry.

- **Interaction and Input:** Developing intuitive and natural interaction methods is crucial for AR and VR. Advancements in input devices and haptic feedback systems can improve user engagement and enable more precise interactions.

- **Content Creation:** The creation of high-quality and compelling AR and VR content remains a challenge. This includes designing realistic virtual environments, creating meaningful interactions, and ensuring that content meets the demands of different industries and applications.

- **Ethical Considerations:** As AR and VR become more prevalent, ethical considerations regarding privacy, data collection, and the impact on society need to be addressed. Striking the right balance between innovation and responsible use is essential.

Conclusion

Augmented Reality and Virtual Reality are revolutionizing the way we perceive and interact with digital information. AR enhances the real world by overlaying virtual content, while VR creates fully immersive digital environments. Both technologies have a wide range of applications, from gaming and entertainment to education, healthcare, and beyond. As hardware and content development continue to improve, AR and VR are poised to reshape numerous industries and transform the way we experience the world around us.

Exercises

1. Imagine you are designing an AR system for a museum. How would you utilize AR to enhance visitors' experience? Provide three examples of how AR could be used to provide interactive and informative exhibits.

2. VR has the potential to revolutionize remote learning and online education. Discuss three ways in which VR can enhance the learning experience and provide advantages over traditional online education methods.

3. The field of medicine has seen significant advancements in the use of AR and VR. Research and discuss one specific application of AR in surgery and one specific application of VR in patient therapy or rehabilitation.

4. Privacy concerns are often raised in relation to AR and VR technologies. Discuss three potential privacy issues that might arise with the widespread adoption of AR and VR and propose possible solutions to address these concerns.

Resources

- *Augmented Reality: Principles and Practice* by Dieter Schmalstieg and Tobias Hollerer provides a comprehensive introduction to the principles, techniques, and applications of AR.

- *Virtual Reality: Concepts and Technologies* by Philippe Fuchs explores the fundamental concepts and technologies behind VR, including hardware, software, and interaction techniques.

- *The Fourth Transformation: How Augmented Reality and Artificial Intelligence Will Change Everything* by Robert

Scoble and Shel Israel offers insights into the future potential of AR and its impact on various industries.

- *Experience on Demand: What Virtual Reality Is, How It Works, and What It Can Do* by Jeremy Bailenson provides an overview of VR technology, its applications, and its social implications.

Fun Fact

Did you know that the term "virtual reality" was coined by Jaron Lanier in the late 1980s? Lanier is considered one of the pioneers of VR and has made significant contributions to the development of this technology.

Challenges and Opportunities in Human Augmentation

Human augmentation, the process of enhancing human capabilities through the integration of technology, offers both exciting opportunities and significant challenges. As advancements in robotics, neurology, and biotechnology continue to progress, the potential for enhancing human abilities becomes more attainable. However, the ethical considerations, social impact, and potential risks associated with human augmentation must also be carefully examined.

Ethical Considerations

The field of human augmentation raises several ethical questions that need to be addressed before widespread adoption. One key concern is the concept of informed consent. Individuals considering augmentation must have a thorough understanding of the risks, benefits, and potential consequences of the procedure. Informed consent becomes even more critical when dealing with experimental or invasive technologies.

Another ethical consideration is the potential for inequality. If human augmentation technologies become accessible only to the wealthy or privileged, it could result in a significant divide between augmented individuals and those who cannot afford the enhancements. This could further exacerbate existing socioeconomic disparities and lead to a "two-tiered" society.

Privacy is also a significant ethical concern in human augmentation. As technologies become more invasive and integrated with the human body, the potential for data collection and surveillance increases. Striking a balance between the benefits of data collection for medical research and the protection of individuals' privacy rights is crucial.

Social Impact

The introduction of human augmentation technologies can have profound social implications. One potential concern is the impact on employment and the workforce. As technologies like robotics and artificial intelligence advance, there is a possibility of job displacement. Augmented individuals with enhanced capabilities may outperform non-augmented individuals, leading to disparities in the job market.

Furthermore, the integration of augmented individuals into society may pose challenges in terms of acceptance and social norms. Society may need to adapt to accommodate individuals with enhanced abilities, addressing issues such as competitive advantages, fairness, and discrimination.

Health and Safety Risks

Ensuring the health and safety of individuals undergoing human augmentation procedures is paramount. It is necessary to thoroughly assess the risks associated with invasive technologies, potential side effects, and long-term implications. Regulatory frameworks must be in place to protect individuals from unethical or unsafe practices.

Additionally, there is a risk of dependency on augmentation technologies. If individuals become overly reliant on their enhancements, it could lead to detrimental effects on their overall well-being. Balancing the benefits of augmentation with maintaining human autonomy and personal agency is a critical consideration.

Integration and Compatibility

Successfully integrating human augmentation technologies with the human body and mind poses significant technical challenges. Ensuring seamless compatibility between the augmented technology and the human system requires interdisciplinary collaboration between engineers, neuroscientists, and medical professionals.

Maintaining long-term functionality and durability of augmentation technologies is also crucial. Implants and devices must be designed to withstand the rigors of everyday life and minimize the risk of complications, such as infection or rejection.

Addressing Challenges

To address the challenges associated with human augmentation, it is essential to establish comprehensive ethical guidelines and regulatory frameworks. These guidelines should ensure informed consent, promote accessibility and affordability, and protect individual privacy and autonomy.

Researchers and developers must prioritize safety and undergo rigorous testing and validation processes before introducing new augmentation technologies. Collaborative efforts between academia, industry, and regulatory bodies can facilitate the responsible development and deployment of these technologies.

Education and public awareness initiatives are crucial to foster understanding and acceptance of human augmentation. Society must engage in open and inclusive discussions to explore the potential benefits and risks associated with these technologies. This will enable us to make informed decisions and shape their ethical and social implications.

Opportunities

Despite the challenges, human augmentation presents numerous opportunities for enhancing human capabilities and improving quality of life. Prosthetic limbs and exoskeletons, for example, can significantly enhance mobility and independence for individuals with physical disabilities.

Brain-computer interfaces offer the potential for direct communication between the human brain and computers, enabling new forms of interaction and control. This technology holds promise in assisting individuals with paralysis or neurodegenerative disorders.

Human augmentation technologies can also lead to advancements in healthcare, such as personalized medicine and targeted drug delivery. By integrating sensors and monitoring devices within the human body, early detection and treatment of diseases become more feasible.

Moreover, human augmentation has the potential to revolutionize entertainment, sports, and gaming industries. Augmented reality and virtual reality applications can create immersive experiences and enhance sensory perception, opening up new possibilities for recreation and leisure activities.

Conclusion

Human augmentation offers exciting opportunities to enhance human capabilities and address various challenges associated with disability, disease, and limitations. However, careful consideration of ethical implications, social impact, and potential risks is necessary to ensure responsible and inclusive development of these technologies. By addressing these challenges head-on, we can unlock the full potential of human augmentation while safeguarding human dignity and well-being in the process.

Emerging Technologies

Edge Computing

Edge computing is a paradigm in computing that aims to bring processing power and storage capabilities closer to the source of data generation. Instead of relying solely on centralized cloud servers for data processing and storage, edge computing distributes these tasks to the network edge, which includes devices such as routers, gateways, and edge servers.

Motivation for Edge Computing

The exponential growth of data generated by devices connected to the internet, such as smartphones, IoT devices, and sensors, has led to an increased demand for real-time, low-latency data processing. Traditional cloud computing models, where data is sent to and processed in remote data centers, may not be suitable for applications that require immediate response times or have stringent bandwidth requirements. Edge computing mitigates these challenges by processing data closer to its source, reducing latency, and relieving network congestion.

Key Concepts

Edge Devices: Edge devices are the endpoints in the edge computing network. These devices include sensors, actuators, mobile devices, routers, and gateways. They collect and process data at the network edge, often in real time.

Edge Servers: Edge servers are intermediate computing nodes located closer to the edge devices. They have higher processing capabilities and storage capacity compared to edge devices. Edge servers act as intermediaries between edge devices and centralized cloud servers.

Fog Computing: Fog computing is a concept closely related to edge computing. It extends the capabilities of edge computing by adding a layer of computing and storage resources between edge devices and centralized cloud servers. Fog computing can provide additional computational power, data caching, and localized analytics.

Benefits of Edge Computing

Reduced Latency: By processing data closer to the source, edge computing reduces the time it takes for data to travel to remote cloud servers and back. This is particularly important for applications that require real-time responses, such as autonomous vehicles, virtual reality, and industrial automation.

Bandwidth Optimization: Edge computing minimizes the need to transfer large amounts of data to remote data centers, reducing bandwidth requirements and network congestion. This is especially beneficial for applications that generate massive amounts of data, such as video surveillance systems and IoT deployments.

Improved Reliability: Edge computing can increase reliability by reducing dependency on centralized cloud servers. With edge devices and edge servers capable of local data processing and storage, applications can continue to function even in the absence of a reliable internet connection.

Enhanced Data Privacy: Edge computing enables data to be processed and stored locally, minimizing the need to transmit sensitive data over the network. This enhances data privacy and security, addressing concerns related to data breaches and compliance with privacy regulations.

Challenges and Limitations

Resource Constraints: Edge devices usually have limited processing power, memory, and storage capacities. Designing efficient algorithms that can run on resource-constrained devices while meeting the required performance criteria is a challenge in edge computing.

Data Synchronization: Edge computing introduces the challenge of keeping data synchronized across multiple edge devices and servers. Ensuring consistency and avoiding data conflicts requires careful coordination and synchronization mechanisms.

Security and Privacy: Edge computing brings new security and privacy concerns. With data being processed and stored at the edge, there is an increased risk of unauthorized access, data leakage, and malicious attacks. Robust security mechanisms and encryption techniques need to be implemented to address these concerns.

Use Cases

Internet of Things (IoT): Edge computing is well-suited for IoT deployments, where a massive number of devices generate data. By processing data locally, edge computing enables real-time analytics, reduces the amount of data transferred to the cloud, and enhances privacy and security.

Autonomous Vehicles: Edge computing plays a critical role in autonomous vehicles by enabling real-time data processing for tasks such as object detection, collision prevention, and decision-making. By reducing latency, edge computing enhances the safety and responsiveness of autonomous vehicles.

Smart Cities: Edge computing is instrumental in building smart city infrastructure, where data is collected from various sensors and devices distributed throughout the city. Edge computing enables real-time analysis and decision-making for applications such as traffic monitoring, energy management, and waste management.

Open Challenges and Future Directions

Performance Optimization: Developing efficient algorithms and optimization techniques that maximize resource utilization while meeting performance requirements is an ongoing challenge in edge computing.

Standardization: Edge computing is a rapidly evolving field with multiple players offering their own solutions. Standardization efforts are needed to ensure interoperability, compatibility, and seamless integration of edge computing systems.

Edge-Cloud Collaboration: Effective collaboration between edge devices and centralized cloud servers is crucial for edge computing infrastructure. Future research should focus on developing mechanisms for efficient data transfer, workload distribution, and coordinated decision-making between edge and cloud resources.

Summary

Edge computing is a distributed computing paradigm that brings processing and storage capabilities closer to the source of data generation. It offers significant advantages such as reduced latency, optimized bandwidth usage, improved reliability, and enhanced data privacy. However, edge computing also presents challenges related to resource constraints, data synchronization, security, and privacy. It finds applications in IoT, autonomous vehicles, and smart cities, among others. Ongoing research focuses on performance optimization, standardization, and edge-cloud collaboration to unlock the full potential of edge computing in the future.

6G Technology and Beyond

As technology continues to advance at an unprecedented pace, we find ourselves on the cusp of a new era: the era of 6G technology. Building upon the foundation laid by 5G, 6G aims to revolutionize communication and connectivity in ways we have yet to imagine. In this section, we will explore the principles, challenges, and potential applications of 6G technology and discuss the future prospects it holds.

Understanding 6G Technology

6G technology refers to the sixth generation of wireless communication networks. While 5G technology enables lightning-fast data transfer speeds and low latency, 6G aims to surpass these capabilities by taking advantage of advancements in various fields, including telecommunications, computing, and data processing. The key principles of 6G technology include:

1. **Hyperconnectivity:** 6G technology will bring about unparalleled levels of connectivity, enabling seamless integration between devices, machines, and humans. It will support massive device-to-device communication and facilitate the Internet of Things (IoT) ecosystem on a much larger scale.

2. **Extreme Data Rates:** One of the defining features of 6G will be its ability to provide even faster data rates than 5G. With speeds expected to reach terabits per second (Tbps), 6G will enable near-instantaneous data transfer, revolutionizing areas such as virtual reality (VR), augmented reality (AR), and holographic communication.

3. **Ultra-Low Latency:** 6G technology aims to reduce latency to a few microseconds, enabling real-time, mission-critical applications such as remote surgery, autonomous vehicles, and smart infrastructure. By minimizing the delay between data transmission and reception, 6G will enhance user experiences and drive innovations across various sectors.

4. **Energy Efficiency:** In an era of increasing energy consumption, 6G technology seeks to optimize power usage. By implementing intelligent network management techniques and leveraging energy-efficient hardware, 6G aims to minimize the environmental impact while still delivering unparalleled performance.

5. **Ubiquitous Coverage:** 6G technology will extend coverage to even the most remote areas, including rural regions and developing countries. Through the use of advanced satellite systems, aerial platforms, and terrestrial networks, 6G aims to achieve ubiquitous and reliable connectivity on a global scale.

Challenges and Solutions

The development and deployment of 6G technology come with a unique set of challenges. Overcoming these obstacles is crucial to harnessing the full potential of 6G. Let's explore some of the key challenges and potential solutions:

1. **Higher Frequencies:** To achieve the desired data rates, 6G will need to exploit higher frequencies in the range of terahertz (THz) and above. However, these frequencies face significant challenges such as increased signal attenuation and limited range. Researchers are exploring advanced antenna technologies, beamforming, and signal processing techniques to address these issues.

2. **Spectrum Availability:** As wireless networks become more crowded, finding sufficient spectrum for 6G becomes a challenge. To overcome this, the utilization of millimeter-wave and terahertz frequencies, as well as novel spectrum-sharing techniques, are being investigated. Additionally, dynamic spectrum allocation and optimization algorithms will play a crucial role in maximizing spectrum utilization.

3. **Security and Privacy:** With the increased connectivity and an exponential growth in connected devices, ensuring the security and privacy of 6G networks becomes paramount. Advanced encryption algorithms, secure and trusted authentication mechanisms, and robust privacy frameworks will be essential to protect against emerging threats and vulnerabilities.

4. **Interference and Reliability:** Achieving seamless connectivity, even in densely populated areas, presents a significant challenge. Interference management techniques, such as coordinated beamforming, interference cancellation, and advanced error correction codes, will be vital to ensure reliable and uninterrupted communication in 6G networks.

5. **Sustainability:** As technology evolves, so does the need for sustainable and eco-friendly solutions. 6G technology

must minimize its environmental footprint by developing energy-efficient hardware, optimizing network architectures, and promoting responsible recycling and disposal practices.

Potential Applications

6G technology has the potential to reshape industries and transform the way we live, work, and interact. Here are some potential applications of 6G:

1. **Extended Reality (XR):** 6G will enable immersive extended reality experiences by providing ultra-high data rates and ultra-low latency. Users will be able to enjoy realistic VR and AR applications, facilitating advancements in gaming, entertainment, education, and remote collaboration.

2. **Autonomous Systems:** With its high reliability, low latency, and massive connectivity, 6G will accelerate the development of autonomous systems. This includes self-driving cars, drones, and robots, which will greatly benefit from real-time communication and coordination with the surrounding environment.

3. **Smart Cities:** 6G technology will fuel the growth of smart cities by enabling the seamless integration of various systems, including transportation, energy, healthcare, and public safety. Real-time monitoring, predictive analytics, and intelligent decision-making will optimize resource allocation and enhance the quality of urban life.

4. **Remote Healthcare:** 6G will revolutionize healthcare by enabling remote surgeries, telemedicine, and remote patient monitoring. Surgeons will be able to perform

complex procedures from a distance, and patients in remote areas will have access to specialized medical care, saving lives and improving healthcare equity.

5. **Connected Industries:** 6G will drive the fourth industrial revolution by enabling massive machine-type communication, industrial automation, and intelligent supply chains. This will enhance productivity, reduce downtime, and enable predictive maintenance in manufacturing, logistics, and other industries.

Conclusion

6G technology represents the next frontier in wireless communication, promising lightning-fast data rates, ultra-low latency, and ubiquitous connectivity. As we embark on the journey towards 6G, it is crucial to address the challenges that lie ahead and leverage this technology responsibly. By doing so, we can unlock a world of new possibilities, revolutionizing industries and transforming the way we live in ways we have yet to imagine.

In the next and final section, we will recap the milestones of computing history and explore the ongoing evolution of computing, as well as the trends shaping its future.

Biocomputing: Merging Biology and Computing

Biocomputing is an emerging interdisciplinary field that combines principles from biology and computing to develop new methods for solving complex problems. This field seeks to harness the power of biological systems, such as DNA and proteins, to perform computations and solve problems that are difficult or impossible for traditional computers.

Background

Computers have traditionally relied on silicon-based technology to process and store information. However, as the demand for computational power and efficiency increases, researchers are exploring alternative approaches. Biocomputing offers a promising solution by leveraging the inherent capabilities of biological systems.

In the world of biology, DNA is a remarkable molecule that carries the genetic information of living organisms. It consists of four nucleotide bases: adenine (A), cytosine (C), guanine (G), and thymine (T). These bases pair with each other in a complementary manner (A with T, and C with G), allowing DNA to store and transmit information.

Principles of Biocomputing

The field of biocomputing is based on several key principles:

1. DNA Computing: DNA molecules can be manipulated to store and process information. In DNA computing, these molecules are used to represent and perform computations on data. DNA strands can be modified through chemical processes to encode information, and DNA-based algorithms can be designed to manipulate and analyze this encoded information.

2. Biochemical Reactions: Biocomputing relies on the use of biochemical reactions to perform computations. These reactions can be engineered to mimic the logic gates used in traditional computing. For example, specific DNA sequences can act as input and output signals, and enzymatic reactions can be used to process and transform these signals.

3. Parallelism: Biological systems inherently operate in parallel, allowing for massive parallel processing. Biocomputing takes advantage of this parallelism by using DNA strands to perform multiple computations simultaneously. By leveraging

the immense information processing capacity of DNA, biocomputing can solve complex problems more efficiently than traditional computers.

4. Biomolecular Data Storage: DNA has the potential to serve as a highly dense and durable data storage medium. The information on DNA can be encoded in the sequences of its nucleotide bases, and advancements in DNA synthesis and sequencing technologies have made it possible to store large amounts of data on DNA molecules. Biocomputing aims to develop methods to read, write, and retrieve information from DNA data storage systems.

Applications of Biocomputing

Biocomputing holds promise for a wide range of applications in various fields, including:

1. Drug Discovery: Biocomputing can be used to model and simulate the interactions between drug compounds and biological targets. By designing DNA-based algorithms and biochemical reactions, researchers can rapidly screen large libraries of drug candidates to identify potential therapeutic molecules.

2. Data Storage: DNA has the potential to store vast amounts of information in a compact form. Applying biocomputing principles, researchers are exploring DNA as a medium for long-term data storage. The high storage density and long-term stability of DNA make it a promising solution for archival storage.

3. Bioinformatics: Biocomputing plays a vital role in analyzing and interpreting biological data, such as DNA sequences and protein structures. By developing computational models based on biological principles, researchers can gain insights into complex biological processes and improve our understanding of living systems.

4. Artificial Life: Biocomputing contributes to the emerging field of artificial life, where researchers aim to create synthetic biological systems that exhibit lifelike behaviors. By integrating computational models with biological components, scientists can engineer living systems with novel functionalities and behaviors.

Challenges and Future Directions

Despite its significant potential, biocomputing faces several challenges that need to be addressed:

1. Scalability: While biocomputing offers massive parallelism, the scalability of biological systems for complex computations is still limited. Efforts are underway to improve the scalability of biocomputing technologies, such as DNA synthesis and sequencing methods.

2. Reliability: Biological systems are prone to errors, such as DNA mutations and enzymatic reactions that may introduce noise in computations. Developing robust error correction mechanisms and improving the reliability of biocomputing systems are areas of active research.

3. Integration with Traditional Computing: Biocomputing is not meant to replace traditional computing but rather to complement it. Integrating biocomputing with existing computing technologies poses technical and practical challenges that require further exploration.

The future of biocomputing holds exciting possibilities. Advancements in DNA synthesis, sequencing, and computing technologies will enable researchers to tackle increasingly complex problems using biological systems. By merging the power of biology and computing, biocomputing has the potential to revolutionize fields such as healthcare, data storage, and artificial intelligence.

Further Reading

1. Lipton, R., & Reggia, J. (1995). DNA-based computing. Scientific American, 273(4), 76-81.

2. Benenson, Y. (2009). DNA computing and molecular programming: an introduction. New York: Springer.

3. Schmidt, M., & Yin, P. (2011). Optimizing stepwise assembly of DNA nanostructures from a macroscopic to a molecular scale. Science, 333(6047), 1662-1666.

4. Goldman, N., Bertone, P., Chen, S., Dessimoz, C., LeProust, E., Sipos, B., ... & Birney, E. (2013). Towards practical, high-capacity, low-maintenance information storage in synthesized DNA. Nature, 494(7435), 77-80.

5. Roque, F. S., Blackburn, J. M., & Beckmann, M. (2019). Towards bio-computational design and manufacturing of functional nucleic acids for a synthetic biology. Synthetic and Systems Biotechnology, 4(1), 1-7.

Summary

Biocomputing represents the integration of biology and computing, leveraging the power of DNA and biochemical reactions to perform computations. It offers potential applications in drug discovery, data storage, bioinformatics, and artificial life. The scalability and reliability of biocomputing systems are areas of active research. As technologies and methodologies advance, biocomputing has the potential to transform numerous fields and contribute to solving complex problems in innovative ways.

Conclusion

Recap of Milestones

Key Events in Computing History

In this section, we will explore some of the key events in the history of computing that have shaped the field and paved the way for the modern digital age. These events have not only changed the way we live and work but also revolutionized the entire world. Let's dive into the fascinating journey of computing and discover the milestones that have brought us to where we are today.

The Invention of the Abacus (3000 BCE)

One of the earliest known computing devices is the abacus, which was invented around 3000 BCE in ancient Mesopotamia. The abacus allowed humans to perform basic arithmetic calculations by sliding beads on rods. While simple in design, the abacus was a breakthrough in early computation and laid the foundation for future developments in numerical systems.

The Antikythera Mechanism (150-100 BCE)

Discovered in a shipwreck off the coast of the Greek island of Antikythera, the Antikythera Mechanism is an ancient analog computer estimated to have been built between 150 and 100 BCE. This remarkable device, consisting of a complex arrangement of gears, was used to track astronomical positions and predict celestial events. The Antikythera Mechanism is a testament to the advanced knowledge and engineering expertise of the ancient Greeks.

The Invention of Calculus (Late 17th Century)

The development of calculus by Sir Isaac Newton and Gottfried Wilhelm Leibniz in the late 17th century marked a significant milestone in the history of computing. Calculus provided a powerful mathematical framework for solving complex problems and laid the groundwork for many subsequent advancements in scientific and computational thinking. The principles of calculus are fundamental to modern computing, particularly in areas such as algorithms and numerical analysis.

The Analytical Engine (1837)

Charles Babbage's Analytical Engine, conceived in 1837, is considered the first general-purpose computer design. Although never fully built during Babbage's lifetime, the Analytical Engine introduced several concepts that are central to modern computing. It employed punched cards for input and output, had a central processing unit (CPU), and could perform arithmetic calculations. Ada Lovelace, a mathematician, and writer, recognized the potential of the Analytical Engine and is credited with writing the first algorithm explicitly designed for a machine.

The Invention of the Telegraph (1837)

The invention of the telegraph by Samuel Morse and Alfred Vail in 1837 revolutionized long-distance communication. The telegraph used electrical signals to transmit messages over long distances quickly. This development not only led to the establishment of global communication networks but also laid the groundwork for future advancements in electrical engineering and telecommunications, which are essential components of modern computing infrastructure.

The Birth of Computer Programming (Mid-20th Century)

The mid-20th century marked a crucial period for the development of computer programming as we know it today. The invention of high-level programming languages, such as FORTRAN (1957) and COBOL (1959), allowed programmers to write instructions in a more human-readable form. This breakthrough enabled the creation of more sophisticated and complex software, making computers more accessible and versatile.

The Advent of Personal Computers (1970s)

The 1970s witnessed the birth of personal computers, a transformative development that brought computing power directly into the hands of individuals. The Altair 8800, introduced in 1975, is widely regarded as the world's first personal computer kit. This milestone paved the way for the subsequent rise of companies like Apple and IBM, who played a crucial role in popularizing and expanding the use of personal computers.

The Internet Revolution (1990s)

The advent of the internet in the 1990s revolutionized the way we communicate, access information, and conduct business. The World Wide Web, invented by Tim Berners-Lee in 1989, provided a user-friendly interface for navigating and sharing information over the internet. This groundbreaking innovation laid the foundation for the emergence of e-commerce, social media, online education, and many other digitized aspects of our lives that we take for granted today.

The Rise of Artificial Intelligence (21st Century)

With the increasing power of computational systems, the 21st century has witnessed significant advancements in artificial intelligence (AI). Machine learning algorithms have enabled computers to learn from data and perform tasks that were once thought to be the exclusive domain of humans. Applications of AI can be found in various domains, ranging from image recognition and natural language processing to autonomous vehicles and healthcare.

The Era of Quantum Computing (Present and Future)

Quantum computing, a field that explores the principles of quantum mechanics to develop new computing paradigms, is one of the most exciting frontiers in the history of computing. Quantum computers have the potential to solve certain problems exponentially faster than classical computers, unlocking new possibilities in areas such as cryptography, optimization, and scientific simulations. While still in its early stages, quantum computing holds the promise of revolutionizing the field of computing once again.

Conclusion

In this section, we explored some of the key events in the history of computing that have shaped the field and influenced the modern world. From the invention of the abacus to the rise of quantum computing, each milestone has contributed to the ongoing evolution of computing technology. Understanding this rich history allows us to appreciate the incredible progress that has been made and inspires us to continue pushing the boundaries of what is possible in the field of computing. As we move forward, we must remain mindful of the ethical and social implications of our innovations, ensuring that computing technology serves humanity's best interests.

Contributions of Notable Figures

The field of computing has been shaped by the brilliant minds and groundbreaking discoveries of many notable figures throughout history. In this section, we will explore the contributions of some of these individuals who have played a significant role in the evolution of computing. Their ideas and inventions have paved the way for the advancements we enjoy today.

1. Alan Turing: Alan Turing, a British mathematician, is often considered the father of modern computing. His groundbreaking work in the field of computability and artificial intelligence laid the foundation for the Turing machine, a theoretical device that represents a general-purpose computer. Turing's concept of the universal machine became the basis for modern computers, as it could simulate any algorithmic computation.

Turing's most significant contribution was his involvement in cracking the German Enigma machine during World War II. He developed techniques to decrypt the encrypted messages used by the German military, which greatly contributed to the Allied victory. This work highlighted the potential of computers in cryptography and laid the foundation for modern-day computer security.

2. George Boole: George Boole, an English mathematician and logician, developed the field of Boolean algebra, which is fundamental to modern computer science. Boolean algebra introduced the concept of binary logic, where variables take on values of either true or false. Boole's work formed the basis for logical operations performed in electronic circuits, such as AND, OR, and NOT gates.

Boolean algebra is deeply integrated into programming languages, data structures, and algorithms. It enables binary representation and manipulation of information, making it possible to perform complex computations in modern computers.

3. Charles Babbage: Charles Babbage, an English mathematician and inventor, is widely recognized as the "Father of the Computer." In the early 19th century, Babbage proposed the concept of the Analytical Engine, a general-purpose mechanical computer. Although the Analytical Engine was never built during his lifetime, it incorporated several key concepts that laid the foundation for modern computers.

Babbage introduced the concept of a stored program, a set of instructions stored in memory that a computer can execute sequentially. His design also included the use of punched cards for input and output, a concept that later influenced the development of early computers.

4. Ada Lovelace: Ada Lovelace, an English mathematician and writer, is celebrated as the world's first computer programmer. Lovelace collaborated with Charles Babbage and wrote the first algorithm intended to be processed by a machine. Her insights into Babbage's Analytical Engine and her ability to understand its potential capabilities led her to envision the use of the machine for more than just number crunching.

Lovelace emphasized the idea that a machine could manipulate symbols and not just numbers, making her a visionary in the field of computing. Today, her contributions are celebrated during Ada Lovelace Day, an annual event that recognizes the achievements of women in science, technology, engineering, and mathematics (STEM).

5. Grace Hopper: Grace Hopper, an American computer scientist, made significant contributions to the development of programming languages and system software. Hopper is best known for her work on the development of COBOL (Common Business-Oriented Language), one of the first high-level programming languages.

Hopper recognized the importance of creating programming languages that could be easily understood by humans, leading to the development of user-friendly and efficient software. Her work had a profound impact on computer programming, making it more accessible and paving the way for future advancements in software development.

6. John von Neumann: John von Neumann, a Hungarian-American mathematician and physicist, made significant contributions to the design and architecture of modern computers. Von Neumann's key idea was the concept of a stored-program computer, where both data and instructions are stored in the same memory.

His von Neumann architecture has become the basis for most computers built since the 1940s. It consists of a central processing unit (CPU), memory, input/output devices, and a control unit, enabling the execution of a stored program.

7. Tim Berners-Lee: Tim Berners-Lee, a British computer scientist, is credited with inventing the World Wide Web. In 1989, Berners-Lee proposed the concept of a distributed information system, allowing documents to be linked together using hyperlinks and accessible through a web browser.

His creation of HTML (Hypertext Markup Language),

HTTP (Hypertext Transfer Protocol), and the first web browser, called WorldWideWeb, revolutionized the way information is accessed and shared globally. Berners-Lee's vision of a decentralized and open web continues to shape the modern internet.

These notable figures have left an indelible mark on the field of computing. Their contributions have significantly advanced the capabilities of computers, shaping the world we live in today. As we continue to push the boundaries of technology, it is essential to recognize and honor the achievements of these pioneers. They have laid the foundation for a future where computing will continue to impact every aspect of our lives.

References: - Campbell-Kelly, M., Aspray, W., Ensmenger, N., & Yost, J. (2014). Computer: A History of the Information Machine. Westview Press. - Ceruzzi, P. E. (2010). Computing: A Concise History. MIT Press. - Grier, D. A. (2013). When Computers Were Human. Princeton University Press.

The Ongoing Evolution of Computing

Trends Shaping the Future

The field of computing is constantly evolving, driven by technological advancements and societal needs. In this section, we will explore some of the key trends that are shaping the future of computing.

Artificial Intelligence (AI) and Machine Learning (ML)

Artificial Intelligence (AI) and Machine Learning (ML) are areas of computing that have gained significant attention in recent years. AI refers to the development of intelligent systems that can perform tasks that normally require human intelligence, while

ML focuses on the development of algorithms that allow computers to learn from data and make predictions or decisions.

One trend shaping the future of computing is the increasing integration of AI and ML into various applications and industries. AI-powered technologies are being used in fields such as healthcare, finance, transportation, and cybersecurity, among others. These technologies have the potential to automate processes, enhance decision-making, and drive innovation.

For example, in healthcare, AI and ML algorithms are being used to analyze medical data, identify patterns, and make predictions for diagnosis and treatment. In finance, AI-powered systems are being used for fraud detection, risk assessment, and algorithmic trading. In transportation, AI is driving the development of autonomous vehicles and smart transportation systems.

However, along with the immense potential of AI and ML, there are also ethical considerations and challenges. Issues such as algorithmic bias, privacy concerns, and the impact of automation on jobs need to be carefully addressed to ensure responsible and beneficial use of AI and ML technologies.

Internet of Things (IoT)

The Internet of Things (IoT) is another major trend that is shaping the future of computing. The IoT refers to the network of physical devices, vehicles, appliances, and other objects embedded with sensors, software, and connectivity, enabling them to collect and exchange data.

The proliferation of IoT devices has led to the generation of massive amounts of data, which can be harnessed to gain insights and drive decision-making. IoT technologies have applications in various domains, including smart homes, healthcare, agriculture, manufacturing, and transportation.

For instance, in smart homes, IoT devices such as smart thermostats, lights, and security systems can be controlled remotely through mobile apps. In healthcare, IoT devices can be used to monitor patients' vital signs remotely and enable proactive and personalized healthcare.

However, the increasing number of connected devices also raises concerns related to data security and privacy. As more devices become interconnected, ensuring the security of data transmission, storage, and processing becomes crucial. Additionally, issues such as interoperability, standardization, and the sustainability of IoT infrastructure need to be addressed for the widespread adoption of IoT technologies.

Cloud Computing

Cloud computing is a paradigm that allows users to access computing resources, such as storage, processing power, and software applications, over the internet. Instead of relying on local servers or personal computers, users can leverage the scalability and flexibility provided by cloud providers.

One trend shaping the future of computing is the continued growth of cloud computing and the transition towards a cloud-based infrastructure. Cloud computing offers numerous benefits, including cost savings, improved scalability, and increased accessibility to computing resources.

Organizations can offload the burden of managing physical hardware and infrastructure to cloud providers, enabling them to focus on their core business activities. Cloud computing also facilitates collaboration and remote work, as users can access their applications and data from any device with an internet connection.

However, as cloud computing becomes more prevalent, challenges such as data security, privacy, and regulatory compliance need to be addressed. Organizations need to ensure that their data is protected and that appropriate security measures are in place to prevent unauthorized access or data breaches.

Edge Computing

Edge computing is an emerging trend that involves shifting computing and data storage closer to the source of data generation, rather than relying on centralized cloud servers. In edge computing, data processing and analytics take place at or near the edge of the network, enabling real-time insights and reducing latency.

Edge computing is driven by the growing demand for low-latency applications and the need to process and analyze data in real-time. This trend is particularly relevant in scenarios where immediate action is required, such as autonomous vehicles, industrial automation, and smart cities.

For example, in autonomous vehicles, edge computing allows for real-time processing of sensor data, enabling quick decision-making and response. In industrial automation, edge computing can enable predictive maintenance by analyzing sensor data in real-time and detecting anomalies.

However, edge computing also poses challenges related to infrastructure, security, and scalability. The distributed nature of edge computing requires robust infrastructure and networking capabilities. Additionally, ensuring data security and privacy at the edge becomes crucial, as data is distributed across multiple devices and locations.

Quantum Computing

Quantum computing is an area of computing that harnesses the principles of quantum mechanics to perform computations that are infeasible for classical computers. Quantum computers use quantum bits, or qubits, which can exist in multiple states simultaneously, thanks to the principle of superposition, and can be entangled with other qubits.

While still in its early stages of development, quantum computing holds the promise of solving complex problems exponentially faster than classical computers. This has significant implications for fields such as cryptography, optimization, drug discovery, and materials science.

However, quantum computing also presents challenges such as qubit stability, error correction, and scalability. Building and maintaining stable qubits is a major technological hurdle, as quantum systems are highly sensitive to environmental noise and decoherence. Additionally, developing error correction methods and scaling up the number of qubits are active areas of research in the field.

Despite these challenges, advancements in quantum computing are expected to have a profound impact on various industries and scientific research, opening up new possibilities for solving complex problems that were previously out of reach for classical computers.

Conclusion

In this section, we have explored some of the key trends shaping the future of computing. From the increased integration of AI and ML into various applications, to the growing influence of IoT, cloud computing, edge computing, and quantum computing, these trends are expected to reshape industries, drive innovation, and solve complex problems.

As computing continues to evolve, it is essential to consider the ethical and societal implications of these advancements. Ensuring the responsible and beneficial use of these technologies requires addressing issues such as data privacy, security, bias, and the impact on jobs.

By staying informed and adapting to these trends, individuals and organizations can harness the full potential of computing and contribute to a future where technology enhances our lives and addresses some of the world's most pressing challenges.

The Interconnected Future of Computing

As we delve into the future of computing, it becomes clear that the trajectory of this field is moving towards a highly interconnected and interdependent landscape. The advancements in technology, especially in the areas of networking, communication, and data sharing, have paved the way for a future where computers are seamlessly integrated into every aspect of our lives. In this section, we will explore the key trends and concepts shaping the interconnected future of computing.

Internet of Things: Connecting the Physical World

One of the most significant developments in computing is the rise of the Internet of Things (IoT), where everyday objects are connected to the internet, enabling them to communicate and share data with each other. This interconnected network of devices opens up immense opportunities for automation, efficiency, and convenience.

The IoT has already found applications in various domains, including home automation, healthcare, transportation, and agriculture. For example, smart homes use IoT devices to control lighting, temperature, and security systems, providing users with remote control and real-time monitoring capabilities. In healthcare, IoT devices can monitor patients' vital signs and send alerts to healthcare professionals in case of emergencies.

The interconnected nature of IoT systems raises various challenges, including security and privacy concerns. With a vast number of devices connected to the internet, there is an increased risk of cyberattacks and data breaches. It is crucial to implement robust security measures and encryption protocols to protect sensitive information and ensure the trustworthiness of the interconnected IoT ecosystem.

Cloud Computing: On-demand Computing Power

Cloud computing has emerged as a game-changer in the world of computing. It refers to the delivery of computing resources, including storage, processing power, and software applications, over the internet. The cloud offers businesses and individuals the ability to access and utilize computing services without the need for costly infrastructure investments.

The future of computing will be deeply intertwined with cloud computing. It enables the storage and processing of vast amounts of data, facilitating data analysis, machine learning, and AI capabilities. Cloud-based services also provide scalability, allowing organizations to seamlessly expand their computing resources as needed.

In addition to offering readily available computing power, the cloud allows for collaboration and seamless integration across different devices and platforms. This interconnectedness unlocks new ways of working and interacting, enabling remote collaboration, online learning, and virtual meetings.

However, as more data and services migrate to the cloud, ensuring data security, privacy, and confidentiality becomes increasingly critical. Robust encryption, access control mechanisms, and data backup strategies are essential to safeguard sensitive information in the interconnected cloud environment.

Artificial Intelligence: Advancing Automation

Artificial Intelligence (AI) is transforming the way we interact with computers and machines, and its impact will continue to grow in the interconnected future of computing. AI technologies, such as machine learning and neural networks, enable computers to learn from data, recognize patterns, and make decisions without explicit programming.

As AI systems become more sophisticated, they will play a vital role in automation and decision-making across various industries. Autonomous vehicles, for example, rely on AI algorithms to navigate and make real-time driving decisions. AI-powered chatbots and virtual assistants are becoming ubiquitous, enhancing customer service and streamlining support processes.

However, ethical concerns, such as the potential for bias and discrimination in AI algorithms, need to be addressed. As AI becomes more intertwined with our daily lives, ensuring fairness, transparency, and accountability in AI decision-making is of utmost importance.

Edge Computing: Processing at the Edge

Edge computing is an emerging trend in the computing landscape that complements cloud computing. It involves processing data closer to the source, at the edge of the network, rather than relying solely on a centralized cloud infrastructure. This approach helps reduce latency, improves real-time decision-making, and reduces the volume of data transmitted to the cloud.

The interconnected future of computing will see an increasing reliance on edge computing for latency-sensitive applications, such as autonomous vehicles, smart cities, and industrial automation. By processing data locally, closer to the devices generating it, edge computing enables faster response times, enhances privacy, and reduces bandwidth requirements.

However, edge computing also presents challenges in terms of managing and securing a distributed network of edge devices. Robust edge computing architectures, coupled with intelligent data management and security protocols, are crucial to harness the potential of this interconnected computing paradigm.

Quantum Computing: Opening New Frontiers

Quantum computing, a field still in its infancy, holds the potential to revolutionize computing as we know it. Unlike classical computers that use bits to represent information as either 0 or 1, quantum computers use quantum bits or qubits, which can exist in states of superposition and entanglement. This unique property of qubits allows quantum computers to perform complex computations much faster than classical computers for certain types of problems.

While the practical applications of quantum computing are still being explored, the interconnected future of computing will likely witness quantum computers being utilized in areas such as cryptography, optimization problems, and simulating complex physical systems. Quantum cryptography, for instance, can provide unbreakable encryption schemes based on the laws of quantum physics.

However, developing stable and error-free qubits and overcoming the decoherence challenge remain significant hurdles in realizing the full potential of quantum computing. Continued research and advancements in quantum hardware and error correction techniques are crucial in making quantum computers a practical reality.

The Interconnected Web of Computing

In conclusion, the future of computing is an interconnected web of devices, services, and technologies. The Internet of Things, cloud computing, artificial intelligence, edge computing, and quantum computing are driving this interconnectivity, transforming the way we live, work, and interact.

As we navigate this interconnected future, it is essential to address the ethical and social implications of these advancements. Privacy concerns, algorithmic bias, cybersecurity threats, and the ethical use of AI are critical challenges that need to be tackled proactively.

The evolution of computing is a continuous journey, and the future prospects are both exhilarating and daunting. The interconnectedness of computers and technology will shape the world in unprecedented ways, and it is our collective responsibility to ensure that these transformations align with our societal values and aspirations.

Index

9 781778 902031

Printed by Libri Plureos GmbH in Hamburg, Germany